INBOUND

CONTENT

INBOUND

CONTENT

A Step-by-Step Guide to
Doing Content Marketing
the **Inbound** Way

JUSTIN CHAMPION

WILEY

Library of Congress Cataloging-in-Publication Data

Names: Champion, Justin, 1986- author.
Title: Inbound content : a step-by-step guide to doing content marketing the inbound way / Justin Champion.
Description: Hoboken : Wiley, 2018. | Includes bibliographical references and index. |
Identifiers: LCCN 2018000766 (print) | LCCN 2018005631 (ebook) | ISBN 9781119488972 (ePub) | ISBN 9781119488965 (ePDF) | ISBN 9781119488958 (hardback)
Subjects: LCSH: Marketing. | Relationship marketing. | BISAC: BUSINESS & ECONOMICS / Marketing / General.
Classification: LCC HF5415 (ebook) | LCC HF5415 .C482433 2018 (print) | DDC 658.8/02–dc23
LC record available at https://lccn.loc.gov/2018000766

Printed in the United States of America

10 9 8 7 6 5 4 3 2 1

Create value before you try to extract it.

—Dharmesh Shah

Contents

Foreword

I must be frank: I have a love/hate relationship with the phrase "content marketing."

Why?

Well, let's start with the hate part.

As a small business owner and entrepreneur, I learned an important reality many years ago: If you want to get something approved in business, you call it "sales." If you want to get it rejected, or at least tabled for another day, you call it "marketing."

Yes, it's the truth. And if you've been in the business world for any period of time, you know exactly what I'm talking about.

No CEO is ever going to wake up one morning and say, "I want to be the best content marketer in the world." Not going to happen.

But once someone gets past the "marketing speak" and truly understands what content marketing is, then there's so much to love. The fact is, I owe all my business success today to the principles of content marketing. But to understand where I'm coming from, you need to know where it all began.

In 2001, fresh out of college, I started a swimming pool company with my two dear friends, Jim Spiess and Jason Hughes. Those early years were quite difficult, but we managed. Over time, we started to figure out who we were and how to be successful. But just when I thought we were finally going to make headway, 2008 happened, and everything changed.

You remember that year, don't you?

In what seemed like an overnight turn of events, the U.S. economy collapsed. Banks were foreclosing. The stock market plummeted. And with it, consumer confidence tanked. The economic collapse of 2008 was brutal for the entire swimming pool industry. Many contractors had to close their doors. Others were forced to make drastic cuts to stay afloat.

River Pools and Spas was by no means immune to this pain. In fact, by January of 2009, my company was staring bankruptcy square in the face. But, as is often the case with trials and tribulation, this incredibly hard period proved to be a godsend. It forced me to finally look around and accept what I already knew: Buyers had changed.

Yes, the Internet had become the ultimate educational source for most consumers. Yet we at River Pools had not yet responded to this digital shift.

It was during this difficult time that I started to throw myself into learning about using the Internet to build my business. I read such phrases as "inbound marketing," "content marketing," "blogging," and many others. But the more I learned about all of this technical jargon, the more my simple "pool guy" mind interpreted everything back to this simple point:

"Marcus, if you obsess over the questions your prospects and customers ask every single day, and you're willing to address those questions honestly, transparently, and consistently on your website through text and video, you just might save your business."

Yes, it was really that simple for me.

I knew our new goal would come down to our ability to teach and communicate with today's digital buyer in a way that would (hopefully) garner trust, traffic, leads, and sales. And, as you might have already guessed, this is exactly what happened.

Over the next two years, despite the difficult economy, somehow we survived as a company.

Not only did we survive, we thrived.

When we became prolific teachers on our website, the traffic and leads started to take off. And as things worked, I became more and more bold.

On our website we addressed any question you could possibly think of with respect to a fiberglass pool, most of which had never been addressed by other swimming pool companies. Whether the question was good, bad, or ugly, we were going to address it, without bias, and with the reader or viewer in mind.

Well, to make a long story short, River Pools landed back on solid ground. And when I say "solid," I mean really solid. In fact, by 2016, we averaged 600,000 visitors a month to our website, making it the most trafficked swimming pool website in the world.

Not only did this explosion in traffic and leads catapult us to be the largest installer of fiberglass pools in the United States, it ended up creating an interesting "problem"—we were getting leads from all over the country, leads that we couldn't service because they were out of our area.

It was at this point we took all the revenue we had built since our digital shift and invested it back into the business, building a manufacturing facility for fiberglass swimming pools.

In 2017, just over a year later, we built roughly 200 fiberglass swimming pools—something unheard of for such a young manufacturer. And within the next 7 to 10 years I expect us to be the largest manufacturer of fiberglass pools in the United States.

So do I love content marketing? Oh, yes. Clearly, I do.

But to reiterate, to me, it's not about marketing. In fact, what we're really talking about here is *trust*.

Trust is the one commonality every business shares. Trust is the battle we're all in. And our ability to gain trust in the marketplace is what content marketing is all about.

So does this book apply to you and your business? Well, if you're in the business of trust, then yes, it does.

But let's say you do buy in to what I'm saying here. What's next? How do you even begin to climb this mountain?

Well that, my friends, is *exactly* why the book you're about to read is so powerful.

In fact, after every chapter you read, you're going to discover action items that you can immediately apply to your business and start getting results from. Pretty cool, huh?

Essentially, what you have here is a textbook. It gives you the framework and corresponding exercise needed to truly *get stuff done*.

And that's exactly why I wanted to write this foreword. Because at this point, no one needs another book that simply "inspires" them. Rather, we need books that help people know exactly what to do, how to do it, and why it matters. Frankly, it's all about action.

That's the essence of *Inbound Content*. And that's why I think this book is so very important for business owners and marketers around the globe to not just read, but embrace.

So read on. Discover the teacher within. And watch the results follow.

Marcus Sheridan
Owner/Partner at IMPACT
Author of *They Ask You Answer*
www.impactbnd.com
twitter.com/TheSalesLion

Preface

I've been a digital marketer for nine years; I've been a Hub-Spotter for four years; and I've been working on the road as a digital nomad for 12 months.

On June 30, 2017, my wife, Ariele, and I completed a 10,700-mile trek. We traveled across the United States in 100 days in our Airstream truck camper.

I'm the content professor for HubSpot Academy. HubSpot Academy's purpose is to educate and inspire people so that we, together, transform the way the world does business. The purpose of this 100-day journey was similar to the Academy's purpose: to educate and inspire people to create more effective inbound content for their businesses. Little did I know that I, too, would be educated and inspired to create something special: a resource that teaches people how to become effective content marketers with activities that actually help them transform into one.

I wrote the first draft in six weeks while we traveled 6,714 miles from Southern California to Front Royal, Virginia. How'd I write it so quickly? I repurposed and expanded teachings from the HubSpot Content Marketing Certification, which I launched in November of 2016. Plus, I channeled my inner Brian Halligan (HubSpot's CEO) and flexed my thinking time more than usual.

Driving 10,700 miles allows for an abundance of reflection time. And I put it to good use. When we weren't traveling, I was writing the content; when we were traveling, I was reflecting on the content and organizing and planning the next steps. Talk about getting some serious stuff done in a short amount of time.

It's not easy living and working from the road, but it is possible and can be rewarding when done with the right mindset. Ariele and I learned a lot from our journey. We even created a page on our website that provides resources and education on becoming a digital nomad: wildwewander.com/digital-nomad. Check out the page if you want to learn more about how to be inspired and create value by working from anywhere and everywhere. *Content marketing can be done from any location.*

As you read this book, take the time to be in the moment. Know that the content came from a good place with a specific intention: to help you and your business grow and succeed. Take in the energy of every word, and immediately apply the knowledge you acquire to your business.

I hope you enjoy reading this book as much as I enjoyed writing it. If you find yourself with questions or just want to say hi, connect and engage with me on Twitter (twitter.com/justinrchampion). I'd love to hear from you.

Acknowledgments

Seek out people who care about what you believe in, and find ways to work with them to create something memorable. The finished product will be more complete than anything you could have created yourself.

The content in this book was a team effort. Big thanks and much love to everyone who contributed in some way, shape, or form. These people include Rachael Perry, Lindsay Thibeault, Guillaume Delloue, Casey Linehan, Joseph Del Bene, Jami Oetting, Kit Lyman, Markiesha Ollison, Tori Zopf, Julie Kukesh, Ty Stelmach, Eric Peters, Chris LoDolce, Ken Mafli, Ryan Malone, David Arnoux, and Sujan Patel.

About the Author

Justin Champion has been a digital marketer for nine years, working with clients like Majestic Athletic, Wrangler Jeans, and Pendleton Whisky. He has always enjoyed building brands that consumers can relate to by creating compelling content. He now works as HubSpot Academy's content marketing professor, which has brought this passion full circle, because he is now able to teach anyone how to grow a successful business through content marketing best practices. Justin is the creator of HubSpot Academy's Content Marketing Certification, which is a globally recognized course.

Justin is a digital nomad—a full-time remote worker who lives and works from the road in his Airstream and truck camper. This book was written during Justin's 2017 U.S. inbound content workshop roadshow. Follow him and his journeys at instagram.com/wildwewander.

Introduction
Your Content Marketing Transformation

Welcome to *Inbound Content*. This book will teach you content marketing concepts that you can apply to your business, turning yourself into a lean, mean content marketing machine.

By the end of this book, you will:

1. Have completed a workbook that will help you get your business's content process up and running.
2. Be prepared to pass the HubSpot Academy Content Marketing Certification final test, earning a valuable industry certification.
3. Be equipped with the knowledge needed to start and maintain a content marketing process for your business.

If you're like me and are a visual learner, *watch the content in video format by signing up for a free HubSpot Academy account*. Sign up for your free account now: hubspot.com/cmc. Ready? Let's do this.

What Is Content Marketing?

Content marketing is a strategic marketing and business process focused on creating and distributing valuable, relevant, and consistent content. This content is meant to attract and retain a clearly defined audience and, ultimately, drive profitable customer action.

Even though content marketing has grown in popularity in the past ten years with the rise of Web 2.0, *content marketing is not a new concept.* Early signs of content marketing date back hundreds of years—from Benjamin Franklin creating his annual *Poor Richard's Almanac* to promote his writing business in 1732 to, more notably, John Deere's ever-popular magazine, *The Furrow.* Deere's publication launched in 1895 and is still running strong today with a dedicated website that has more than 38,000 inbound links.[1]

And although the medium has evolved over time, the framework for content marketing is pretty much the same. *It's all about your audience, what they value, and how you can help educate and entertain them.* When done correctly, content marketing creates a relationship with your audience that leads to trust. And if your audience trusts you, they'll be more willing to do business with you when they're ready to make a purchase decision.

To communicate with your audience, they need to first find you online. And for your audience to find you online, you need to publish content. *The process of being found (and achieving results), however, is a marathon, not a sprint.* There's a lot of consistent conditioning needed to achieve success. As an example, see Figure I.1 for a graphic of data security company

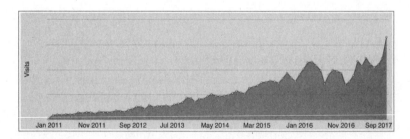

Figure I.1

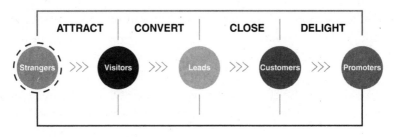

FIGURE I.2

Townsend Security's organic, nonpaid traffic coming from search engines.

Townsend Security created content consistently, for years. *Their results grew over time, not overnight.* The process was similar to that of a marathon, not a sprint.

This company is not alone in understanding how content can help grow their business. Although content marketing costs 62% less than outbound marketing, it generates more than 3 times as many leads.[2] Think about that for a minute.

Content has the important job of pulling people from one stage of the inbound methodology to another.

It plays an integral part in the attract, close, convert, and delight stages (see Figure I.2).

Your content should attract the right people to your site, convert those people into leads, and nurture and help close them into customers. But it doesn't stop there—your content should delight your customers, turning them into promoters of your brand.

In a nutshell, content marketing is really just the art of communicating with your prospects and customers without having to sell to them. Instead of marketing or advertising your products and services, you're creating helpful, entertaining content that your prospects and customers can enjoy and learn from.

If it sounds like inbound marketing and content marketing are similar, that's because they are. They both focus on empowering potential customers, building a lasting relationship with your audience, and creating valuable content that both entertains and educates them.

But what's the difference between the two, and do you need both?

Think in terms of "and" not "or" when it comes to the content marketing–inbound marketing relationship. Success relies on both. Content may help fuel your inbound engine, but there are similarly valuable inbound projects—like technical search engine optimization, product or services trials, marketing automation, and interactive tools—that may exist outside the scope of a content marketer. This is where inbound marketing comes in as a valuable counterpart.

If you aren't opening yourself up to the wide range of inbound practices, you're limiting the potential growth and impact you can have as a marketing leader. In other words, your inbound plan should be a superset—inclusive of your content assets but not limited to them.

It's important to know the landscape of the journey you're about to embark on in this book. Let's review each chapter and get a sense of what you'll be learning.

How Do You Create an Effective Content Marketing Framework for Your Business?

Now that you know how content marketing can help you build a better relationship with your prospects and customers, what steps should you take to create a successful content marketing plan?

You'll start off by learning how to create a content creation framework in your organization. If you really want to create great content, you need to have a process in place that's more advanced than just writing and publishing content. You need to be able to identify campaigns, set timelines, and review and edit content before it goes live, all of which will be discussed in Chapter 1.

You'll also learn about the tools and responsibilities of team members needed to build a successful framework for creating content.

Once you've built this framework, you'll learn about the power of storytelling in Chapter 2.

We just talked about how content marketing is about a relationship. Every company has a story—you need one to survive. What do you stand for? What message do you support? These are all concepts we'll discuss.

Then, once you understand how important storytelling is to content marketing, you'll learn how to generate content ideas to support your content creation efforts. One of the differences between good and great content marketers is that the great ones have a process they rely on to consistently produce high-quality content ideas.

In Chapter 3, you'll learn the techniques to research and uncover an idea and expand on it, whether you're doing it yourself or with a team. Sometimes ideas aren't easily apparent.

Once you're confident in generating content ideas, you'll learn how to plan your long-term content strategy.

In Chapter 4, you'll learn how to create realistic goals for your audience, also known as your buyer personas. You'll learn to perform an audit that will identify content needs and gaps to build a helpful, relevant journey for your personas. You'll also learn how to create your long-term content plan by mapping your content creation road map. This way, you're not wasting gas and you can focus on getting to your destination while circumventing roadblocks along the way.

Once you've learned how to plan a long-term content strategy, you'll learn how to become an effective writer.

In Chapter 5, you'll learn how we get ideas out of our heads and format them into effective pieces of content. Additionally, you'll learn some grammatical pitfalls to avoid. Sometimes a simple incorrect use of "it's" and "its" can deter your audience.

Once you've learned how to become an effective writer and you're ready to start creating content, you'll learn how to create an effective blog post.

In Chapter 6, you'll learn how to format your content in a way that communicates what you're trying to say to search engines while keeping the reader's experience in mind.

Once you've learned how to create a blog post, you'll learn how to extend the value of your content by repurposing it.

In Chapter 7, you'll learn how to proactively identify repurposing opportunities before a piece of content is created, as well as how to repurpose content after it has been created.

You'll also learn how to republish the same content across multiple platforms—a great way to extend the value of your top-performing content.

Once you've learned how to repurpose a piece of content, you'll learn how to effectively promote it.

In Chapter 8, you'll learn how to promote content through distribution channels like email and social media. We'll show you specific tactics to promote your content while making sure you're effective in your approach.

Next, you'll learn how to analyze and measure your content.

Chapter 9 will help you understand various metrics and data points you can track and measure to see if your initiatives are successful. This way, both you and your business will be constantly growing and learning.

You'll also learn how to communicate the results of your content efforts to the rest of your team.

Once you've learned how to analyze and measure the impact of your content marketing efforts, you'll learn how to develop a growth marketing mentality.

In Chapter 10, you'll learn how to instill a growth marketing mindset in your organization and how to manage your growth funnel. This is especially important with the ever-changing landscape of digital media.

Once you've finished Chapters 1–10, *you'll be ready to take the HubSpot Academy Content Marketing Certification final exam*, earning yourself a valuable industry certification and joining a network of more than 112,000 (and growing) certified professionals that are transforming the way the world does business with HubSpot Academy.

But you won't stop there; once you've acquired the knowledge needed to create an effective content marketing process, you'll be ready to learn about topic clusters and pillar pages, which will take your content process to the next level.

Search engines and the habits of searchers are changing. We're in an age in which people want to binge content; they want it now and lots of it.

In Chapter 11, you'll learn how to construct an ungated website page with a relevant conversion point, thereby creating the best experience for searchers as well as search engines.

We've got a lot to cover, so let's get to it.

Chapter 1

Building a Content Creation Framework

Why Does Your Business Need a Framework for Creating Content?

Content marketing, like project or product management, can take a lot of work and time to do right. From creating long-term content plans to analyzing the results, it can be challenging to keep track of all the moving pieces and make sure your work is driving you toward your team and company's goals.

Going through those steps—from the first long-term plan to analyzing the results—can feel laborious and complicated, but it doesn't have to. Having a framework in place that's repeatable, organized, and agile can make the process of creating content much smoother and more rewarding.

When you're creating content on a large scale, you shouldn't have to reinvent the wheel with each piece. Instead, have a clear and repeatable process in place that allows you to produce blog posts, e-books, webinars, and more, all in an efficient manner.

Most content marketers wear a lot of hats, leaving them strapped for time. Having a clear action plan that can be

Thank you to Casey Linehan for your contribution to this chapter.

reused saves time and keeps you and your initiatives moving forward.

A major component of any action plan is organization.

When looking at your long-term content plan, it's important to break up the large goals into digestible chunks that can be completed on a short-term basis. This way, you can make more sense of your content creation needs by listing out the details of what goes into them. For example, if your goal is to create an ebook, focus on the content needed to bring it to life. This can paint a better picture of your weekly content tasks (i.e., blogging, posting on your social channels, etc.).

In addition to being repeatable and organized, your framework should be agile. Business needs and context change over time. When you're planning your initiatives up to a year in advance, it's important to remain flexible to account for the changes that will inevitably arise during the coming months. Sometimes campaigns, timelines, and goals will need to be adjusted.

Now that we've talked about the value of having a content creation framework, let's move on to building that framework.

How Do You Build a Framework for Creating Content?

Here are eight steps to building a content creation framework of your own.

1. Conceptualize your content.
2. Plan and set timelines.
3. Create a content workflow.
4. Review and edit your content.
5. Publish and promote.

6. Organize your content internally.
7. Analyze the results.
8. Evolve your process.

START BY CONCEPTUALIZING YOUR CONTENT

Coming up with ideas may sound like an easy task. But turning an idea into a piece of content is a different story.

The first step your framework should include is the process of coming up with appropriate ideas. If you're struggling to generate content ideas, check out online resources like the HubSpot Blog Ideas Generator and publications related to your industry.[1]

Some other options include writing down frequently asked sales questions or important industry knowledge that might be helpful for your target market to know, or performing keyword research to identify top terms used by people searching for content relevant to your industry. These are topics we'll dig into deeper in Chapter 3.

When creating content, it's important to keep two things in mind:

♦ Your buyer personas
♦ The buyer's journey

Buyer personas are semifictional representations of your ideal customer based on quantitative and qualitative analysis. What that means is you have a business you work for, and that business has products and services it's trying to sell, and those products and services are meant to attract a specific audience (also known as your buyer personas).

Each buyer persona will experience the buyer's journey, which is the active research process a potential buyer goes through leading up to making a buying decision.

The buyer's journey is made up of three stages:

1. **Awareness stage:** The buyer identifies there's a problem that's happening. This person is performing research to learn more and find a possible solution.
2. **Consideration stage:** This person has found one or more solutions to their problem. Now they're looking for the solution that best meets their needs.
3. **Decision stage:** This person is ready to make a well-informed decision, which is usually purchasing a specific product or service.

Following is an example of how a buyer persona might progress through the buyer's journey:

Awareness stage: I have a lot of unstructured text data and need to make sense of it. What should I do?

Consideration stage: Aha! There's an automated solution to categorize comments and detect emotions in real time in multiple languages.

Decision stage: I can receive a free consultation of my business's customer feedback data.

We'll review buyer personas and the buyer's journey in more detail in Chapter 4. For now, keep in mind that content should always support both. If it doesn't, you need to ask yourself why you're creating it in the first place.

Next, Plan and Set Timelines for Content Creation

Once you've established some ideas for content offers, *start planning your timeline, which shouldn't extend more than three months out.* By not planning more than one quarter ahead, you'll be able to maintain agility—things may change over time—while still having time to execute on your initiatives.

We'll discuss content frequency and how extensive your time-line should be in Chapter 4.

When planning short-term content tasks over the span of a quarter, try to have at least two or three major content offers you want to create, and organize them by stage of the buyer's journey. Knowing which content offers to focus on each month will help you organize your weekly content tasks in support of your overall plan. For example, is this offer going to be a webinar or an ebook, and will it be targeted toward the Awareness or Decision stage?

In addition to the process of planning your content offers, you'll want to identify any company-wide initiatives that will need support from content during the next three months. Examples of additional content you might want to include could be posts on trade shows you'll be attending, rebranding information, new corporate partnerships, and various events. Many of these posts will be about sharing company updates, but they might not be about the problems your buyer persona has and the solutions your buyer persona needs.

NEXT, CREATE A WORKFLOW FOR CONTENT CREATION

Your workflow should clearly identify who's going to be doing what tasks. It should also mention any outside influencers who will be contributing and, if so, in what capacity. Your workflow should clearly break down the work to ensure everyone is on the same page. For example, instead of having "written," "edited," and "published" as the work stages for an ebook, you might have something similar to the following checklist:

♦ Outline completed
♦ First draft completed
♦ Editing completed
♦ Design and formatting completed
♦ Final draft completed
♦ Published

Then Review and Edit Your Content

With the content you've now created, you'll need a review system that double-checks if the content has been edited, ensuring search-engine optimization (SEO) best practices have been implemented and the voice, tone, and style of your writing matches your brand's style guide.

Depending on your team and infrastructure, this review process could involve getting authorization to publicly release your content, getting an SEO specialist to format and update the content, or even working with your technical team to make the appropriate updates to your website. *Anticipating who might be involved in the review process will help you avoid any unwanted delays as you make the best content possible.*

To get started creating a process to review and edit content, there are six best practices to keep in mind:

1. Set clear expectations.
2. Allow for multiple rounds of edits.
3. Make suggestions by tracking changes.
4. Determine an editing timeline.
5. Use a document to track progress.
6. Clearly define the roles in the review process.

First, set clear expectations for every time someone reviews a piece of content. The goal is to ensure the reviewer knows what they're looking for, whether it be grammatical errors, fact-checking, story gaps, choice of words, optimizing the content for search engines, or whatever else.

Second, make sure you allow for multiple rounds of edits. When it comes to editing content, you'll want to have between two to four rounds of edits before publishing. *Each round of edits should have clear expectations.* For example, the first round of edits could focus on fact-checking and story gaps, the second round could focus on grammatical errors and optimizing content for search engines, and the third round could be the final look to make sure everything is polished and ready to release into the world.

Third, you should have your content reviewers make suggestions by tracking changes as opposed to making edits directly. This way, the content writer knows where to make changes instead of having to figure out what was altered.

Fourth, determine an editing timeline. A timeline should account for multiple rounds of edits as well as the finished product. The goal of a timeline is to keep everything on schedule and pace so your content production is consistent.

Fifth, use some sort of document, like a google sheet, to track progress. It's important to understand where your content is in the review process. This document should reflect the editing rounds you've determined for your review process.

For example, let's say you're remodeling your kitchen, and you know you have a lot of work to do, from electrical to hanging drywall. Since there's a team of people working together on a final product, how would you know if all the tasks have been completed if you weren't tracking progress? The same goes for reviewing and editing content.

Lastly, clearly define the roles in the review process. This way, everyone knows who's doing what and when. This will help keep things running smoothly.

PUBLISH AND PROMOTE YOUR CONTENT

Now that your content has been created and reviewed, it's time to publish and promote it. Publishing your content is fairly simple—you just need to take the associated website, landing, or blog page(s) live. That being said, you'll want to determine a publishing schedule that accounts for content frequency. This includes time of day, day of the week, and how often you publish content. Remember to keep your buyer personas in mind when determining a publishing schedule.

Promoting content, however, takes a little more fore-thought, because there are multiple channels like email, social media, and so on to consider. In addition to identifying what tone and messaging you want to communicate on each chan-nel, you'll need to identify how you want to drive people to your new content from the rest of your site. This means identifying key places on other relevant website pages that can be used to refer that page's traffic to your new content.

Your promotion strategy should change to reflect your business's needs. This might mean changing the conversion paths you're most heavily promoting on a frequent basis. For example, promoting a content offer that's directed toward a specific persona on your home page might be fully aligned with your business goals one quarter, but if your business's target market shifts in the next, you'll want to update the offer to reflect the changing needs.

ORGANIZE YOUR CONTENT INTERNALLY

Once you've reached the point where you've finished some content, you'll likely have additional landing pages, images, and other associated content that you're storing in your content management system, also known as a CMS.

Whether you're using a traditional CMS like WordPress or HubSpot or using a document storage system like Dropbox or Google Drive, organizing those files in a way that's easy to understand will be critical for successfully repurposing, reus-ing, and even simply finding that content down the line. One easy way to organize your content is by developing a clear nomenclature system. A sample system could include:

+ Content format
+ Buyer's journey stage

- Campaign name
- Year

Let's say you created an awareness-stage ebook in 2016 to support a campaign for a new product launch on rock climbing gear. The nomenclature for hosting this piece of content could look like this: ebook-awareness-rockclimbinggear-2016.

Although you can choose a specific naming convention formula for hosting your files, the *goal should be to easily access files when you need to.*

ANALYZE YOUR CONTENT'S RESULTS

Now that you've planned, created, edited, published, promoted, and organized your content, you need to measure the results to see what insights you can learn.

We'll spend more time talking about how to effectively analyze your content marketing results later, but the basic points are that you'll want to know if your content successfully captured new leads and if those leads went on to continue through the inbound methodology to become customers.

Knowing the answers to those questions will help you determine if your content offers are compelling to visitors and if they successfully create engagement that drives sales.

EVOLVE YOUR PROCESS

The final element of your content creation framework is that it should always be evolving.

Your business's content and goals will vary from quarter to quarter and from year to year, so your content creation process should reflect your organization's processes. Furthermore, content marketing is always changing, so it'll be important to keep on top of industry trends and best practices so that you can incorporate them into your framework appropriately. The following is a list of brands to monitor to stay up to date on the latest content marketing trends:

blog.hubspot.com

contentmarketinginstitute.com

blog.kissmetrics.com

moz.com/blog

contently.com/strategist/

marketeer.kapost.com

searchengineland.com

marketingprofs.com/opinions/

What Resources Do You Need to Build a Content Creation Framework?

You'll need to use two types of resources to create great content.

1. Your team
2. Your tools

Start with Your Team

There are five primary types of responsibilities covered in content creation:

1. Content management and strategy
2. Writing
3. Editing
4. Designing
5. Publishing and promoting

Content management and strategy is the foundational responsibility. This role involves creating a long-term content plan, mapping it to meet the needs of the business, ensuring the other four responsibilities are met, and analyzing performance reports. Most businesses hire a content marketing manager or content marketing strategist to fill this roll.

The second responsibility is actually creating the content, which is typically done by a content marketer or content writer/producer. Although many businesses have niche and/or technical markets, *the people writing your content don't always have to be subject matter experts.* Instead, much like a journalist, they can work with internal and external subject-matter experts to create compelling and useful content. Although many companies choose to write their content in-house, many elect to outsource that work. There are a lot of agencies like Scripted, WriterAccess, and BlogMutt that can help create tailored content for your needs.

Once the content has been planned and created, it will need to be edited to align with your business's messaging, your readers' needs, and the goals the content is working toward. Just because a piece of content has been created doesn't mean it's ready to be published. Before publishing content, make sure it meets your quality standards, is grammatically correct, and communicates your message clearly and concisely.

Once the content has been created, it needs to be packaged in a way that is appealing to readers. Having an attractive, fluid format and design can make all the difference in getting someone to fill out a form for your content and invest time in reading it.

Think about it: Can you remember a time when you looked at a website or flyer and decided not to read it because the format was challenging to understand or didn't visually make sense? In marketing, we call that the blink test. *The average site visitor spends about three to five seconds scanning a website* before deciding if they want to spend time looking through it.[2]

Okay, so now that we've covered the responsibilities of content management and strategy, writing, editing, and designing, **we need to coordinate the publishing and promotion of that content**. When promoting content on social media channels like LinkedIn, Facebook, and Twitter, the marketing coordinator or social media manager is in charge of listening to and engaging with the audience. This role is also responsible for publishing new content, whether to the blog, website, or social media platforms.

Depending on your team and business's context, you might have one person fulfill multiple roles. A good example of this is when a content creator who serves as an editor also has a background in basic design. However, it's important to ensure this person isn't strapped with too much responsibility. As a rule of thumb, *one person should not take on more than two to three responsibilities at a time*. It's important to have a checks and balances system spread among multiple teammates.

However you choose to assemble your team, its primary focus should be on ensuring that whatever content you produce, regardless of quantity, is high-quality work.

Gather Your Tools

Now that we've covered what—or, rather, who—goes into a content marketing team, let's review the tools you'll need to start managing your content.

First things first: You'll need a content management system (CMS) to create, edit, and publish your content. There are different types of content systems, so you'll need to identify which kind works best for your company's needs.

HubSpot is a great example of a system you can use to build, edit, and host content files, and publish blog posts and landing pages. Additionally, HubSpot can host your entire website, making it a one-stop shop for managing your website, marketing, sales, and customer success efforts.

WordPress and Squarespace are also great content management systems to consider—they both help you build, manage, and host your digital content. WordPress, specifically, offers various plugins that extend and expand the functionality of your website.

Whichever CMS you use, you'll want the ability to edit your website, create and publish content on your blog and landing pages, and optimize your content for search engines. Every CMS offers different options, so research them well to make sure the one you choose meets your business's needs.

The second requirement you'll have for these tools is the ability to understand what's happening on your website. Basically, you'll need analytics tools that will show you the impact content has on your business and identify opportunities for improvement.

Both HubSpot and Google Analytics are strong choices for reporting. In fact, I generally recommend companies use both since the two platforms offer different kinds of insights that, combined, help to create a complete picture.

Let's unpack that a bit.

Google Analytics[3] is a great option for understanding exactly where leads are coming from, what kind of device they're using, and how long they're staying on your pages. You can also pull custom, granular reports on your site's traffic, all of which can be used to manage a highly optimized site to give you the best chance of being found online and converting your leads.

HubSpot's analytics[4] really shine in helping you understand where that traffic is coming from and how it's feeding your content marketing funnel. It helps you understand which sources are converting into leads or customers and their various conversion rates through the context of your sales and marketing funnel.

The good news: *You can access both platforms for free.*

Once you have your CMS and analytics ready to go, you'll need something to help with your planning and internal communication. You'll want to make sure your team can communicate easily, see any updates, avoid version- or draft-control issues, and clearly delineate their responsibilities and assignments.

Google Drive[5] is a great example of a tool that can meet each of those needs with shared files, which include the ability to comment, to see previous drafts and edits for version control, and to know who's working on what from any computer with Internet access. Plus, if you live on the road as I do, and Wi-Fi connections can sometimes be limited, you can access and make updates to your files offline. Then, once you're back online, it'll update the files accordingly for all to see.

So, there you have it. We've now covered the importance of a content creation framework, what a framework could look like, and the resources required to create your new content from both a tool and team perspective. By following these steps, you should be able to create your own framework to plan, develop, and publish content campaigns for your business.

Chapter 1 Homework

ACTIVITY 1

It's important to have a real-time, collaborative platform that hosts files in the cloud. Luckily, Google Drive can give you this for free.

1. If you don't already have one, go create a Google Drive account by following this link: https://www.google. com/drive/.

2. If you're new to Google Drive, then review this resource to get started: http://bit.ly/2GfOniC.

ACTIVITY 2

You might have created a piece of content, but that doesn't mean it's ready to be shared with the world—not just yet. Content needs a review system that double-checks if it's been edited, if SEO best practices have been implemented, and if it matches your brand's style guide.

A content review process should include the following:

♦ A defined content creation and approval roles to create accountability and ensure alignment of responsibilities (content creators, reviewers, editors, etc.).

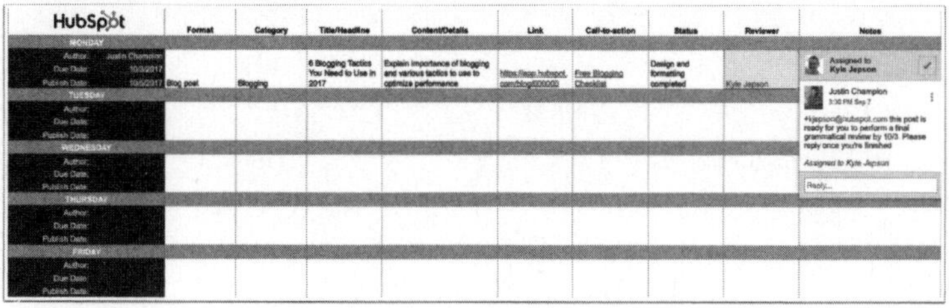

FIGURE 1.1

♦ A defined content creation and approval process before publishing content (rounds of approval with specific details for each round).

♦ A document that tracks the content creation and approval process based on deadlines (helps organize content creation efforts, which keeps content production consistent and on time).

Open a new Google Sheet and outline a content review process for your business.

Figure 1.1 shows a sample outline of a content review process to get you started. Follow this link to access the template: bit.ly/2xa0zzC.

ACTIVITY 3

Having a clear nomenclature for your media is key to staying organized.

Here is a sample nomenclature for an awareness-stage ebook created in 2016 to support a campaign for a new product launch on rock climbing gear: ebook-awareness-rockclimbing-gear-2016.

Open a new Google Doc and create an example nomenclature for the next offer you plan to create and host on your website.

Chapter 2

The Power of Storytelling

Why Does Your Business Need a Story?

Everyone loves a great story. People want to feel connected to a group, to belong. Stories give you a reason to communicate and relate; stories are stimulating and give you something to believe in; stories make you feel better, smarter, safer, or even loved.

Business storytelling is similar. It's about creating alignment between your business and your prospects and customers.

But telling your brand's story is more than what you write on your website, your blog, or even social media. *It's your value and your mission*, and it's how you communicate that consistently to your audience—wherever they are.

Thanks to smartphones and tablets, the average adult spends more than 20 hours per week with digital media.[1] And Google processes over 5.4 million searches per minute.[2]

Wow, 5.4 million search queries per minute? That's a lot of people looking for answers. But capturing their attention can be difficult.

Content marketers are constantly battling for the attention of their prospects and customers. To make sure you're heard,

Thank you to Lindsay Thibeault for your contribution to this chapter.

you need to be genuine and tell a story that appeals to your audience.

Your goal is to make a human connection. It's about resonating with people—people who need your help or guidance.

In the world of business, a story helps you create contrast between choices. Stories will help your prospects make sense of decisions they're about to make, whether it's deciding on a product or service or making a purchase.

Chances are, you're not the only business that does what you do. To survive in today's crowded information market-place, you need to stand out. This is where your business's story comes in.

Stories make your prospects the main characters and can even change the way they think and feel. And storytelling is used in all formats of content. It isn't just used in a lengthy ebook. You can use storytelling in blog posts, email, videos, case studies, guides . . . the list goes on.

So, if a story can be the foundation of all types of content, what's *not* a story?

A story is not just your business's history. A story is why you're doing what you're doing, and telling it in a way that appeals to your audience.

It's also not cliche, it's not what everyone else is saying. Sure, you may think you provide the best customer service in your industry, but that's not your story. *Storytelling is about standing out, not blending in.*

Many companies play it safe and use data, benefits, and return on investment to attract customers, which is important. But logic is rarely appealing and remembered. On the other hand, *emotion is remembered.* Emotion gets shared. And it's not developed by saying "We're the best." It's more about appeal-ing to the emotional side of your prospects and customers than the logic of what you do.

Stories are how your audience remembers. And to help your audience remember, you need to:

- ◆ Stand out by telling a story with the right context.
- ◆ Create contrast by being consistent and authentic.
- ◆ Be conversational to elicit emotion from a specific audience.

As a content marketer, use stories to engage and, most importantly, teach your audience.

How Do You Develop the Structure of Your Story?

First, it's all about how you frame the story you're trying to tell. You need to keep your audience and tone in mind, but, to really nail your branding story, you need to understand the golden circle.

Yes, the Golden Circle. Sounds mysterious, right?

Simon Sinek is an ex–advertising executive and author who is best known for his concept—Golden Circle.

The Golden Circle is all about starting with why.

According to Sinek, most people communicate by starting with what they do and eventually work their way back to talk about how and why they do what they do.

But companies that are universally identified as unique and successful—think Apple or Google—*communicate with an "inside-out" type of thinking*. They start with the why and only then do they move on to talk about the how and what portions of what they do.

You can think about it this way: *Why* do you do what you do? *How* will this help your audience? And *what* are you actually offering?

So, why does the order in which you communicate the story matter? It has to do with the parts of the brain.

When you're talking about what you do, you're speaking to an analytical part of the brain. But when you talk about the why and how, you're communicating with feelings and dealing with human behavior. And remember, storytelling is all about making that connection.

When you're planning a story, take time to think through the way you're choosing to tell it. To really connect with your prospects and customers, express the why of your story. Tap into the emotional side and begin to educate or build awareness from there.

The Golden Circle can help you create your mission statement and set the tone for all your content.

Now that you understand the basic structure of a story, it's important to discuss the elements that make up that story. Regardless of the story you're trying to tell and how you're trying to tell it, storytelling has three essential elements:

1. Character
2. Conflict
3. Resolution

But how do these three parts relate to storytelling and content marketing?

LET'S START WITH YOUR CHARACTERS

With any good story, there are characters. Every story revolves around at least one character. *With content marketing, the people—or characters—are your readers.* Storytelling can't happen without valuing and understanding your audience and responding to their wants and needs.

If potential customers can get the answers to their questions and see themselves as characters in your story, they'll be more likely to use your product or service and experience the happy ending you offer.

Take a second. Think about a piece of content (maybe a blog post) that resonated with you.

Are you thinking about it?

Okay.

Why is this piece of content so memorable?

There may be a few reasons why, but some of the most memorable pieces of content (or stories) stick in an audience's mind because of the characters involved.

For the content you were thinking of, were you the character in the story? Did it resonate with you because you felt like it answered a question? Helped solve a problem?

The character acts as the connection between you, the storyteller, and your audience.

To make sure you're focusing on the right characters, start with your buyer persona. This semifictional representation of your ideal customer can help guide you through understanding the goals and challenges your character will face.

Is your buyer persona a full-time parent? Well, you might know that time is not on their side and they would describe themselves as busy. You should keep that in mind for your story.

Or is your buyer persona a business owner who's looking for a better way to communicate between her team members? She'll likely see herself as the character if a team is used in the stories.

Or maybe you're an education organization looking to attract students who want to take online courses. They might want to read about success stories of students who are just like them.

No matter who your buyer persona is, the art of storytelling is making sure you empathize with and relate to your audience.

While keeping your buyer persona in mind, you should also determine the point of view your story will have. Will it be first person, second person, or third person? There's no right or wrong option. It will depend on your buyer persona, the story you're trying to tell, and the format of that story.

In the first-person point of view, the character is yourself. When you say, "I saw this" or "I learned that," you're speaking in the first person. Using this type of language in storytelling is confessional. It can help you establish a personal connection with the reader. You can use this to build authority. Try using first person when there's a known person, an author, behind the content. This could work for a blog post, video, or even an ebook if the author is noted.

As for second person, the character in this point of view is your audience. It's the point of view used when you say things like "You'll see" or "You'll learn." When using "you" language, you need to understand your buyer personas. Make it personal for them by knowing their pain points, their goals. Tell the story in a way that shows empathy.

Lastly, we can't forget about third person. This is the "he said"/"she said" type of language. Think back to that buyer persona example for an education organization. That buyer persona could potentially benefit from a story written in the third person. Case studies about your customers are a good example of using third person. Stories for this point of view can be either fictional or nonfictional.

Again, there's no right or wrong when it comes to point of view. Keep your buyer personas at the top of your mind and think through what will work best for them.

Most importantly, when it comes to point of view, decide on one and keep it consistent. *Consistency is key when it comes to content and storytelling.*

Next Is Understanding Your Conflict

Once you have an idea of who the character is for your story, it's important to understand the conflict he or she faces.

Your conflict is the lesson in how the character transforms through a challenge. The emphasis here is on "lesson." Remember, when it comes to content marketing and storytelling, the power is in what you're teaching.

TOMS is a slip-on shoe company that focuses on spreading social good; with every product you purchase, TOMS will donate a pair of shoes to a child in need. They've made this a part of their brand identity by creating a slogan that reinforces who they are and what they're about: "The One for One Company."

Now let's break down TOMS's story into three parts.

Everyone needs shoes to protect their feet.

But not everyone has the money to pay for shoes. While traveling in Argentina in 2006, TOMS founder Blake Mycoskie (the story's character) witnessed the hardships children face growing up without shoes.

TOMS is striking an emotional chord with their audience by raising awareness for an issue they're passionate about.

The best part is how TOMS ties it all together with their resolution: If you buy a pair of their shoes, they'll donate a pair of shoes to a child in need.

Now that's a powerful story. And although TOMS started off as a shoe retailer, they've created a big, emotional feel-good story that makes their customers feel like they're changing the world by simply purchasing a pair of shoes. And just how much success has this brought TOMS? Well, they've sold over 60 million pairs of shoes, which means they've also given over 60 million pairs of shoes to children in need.

BEST PRACTICES

Beyond the three elements that make up the story, there are also some best practices to keep in mind.

To make your story effective and relatable to your audience, you'll need to:

- ◆ Use content to create emotional appeal.
- ◆ Be consistent and authentic.
- ◆ Keep the story clear and concise.

USE CONTENT TO CREATE EMOTIONAL APPEAL

Your story needs emotional resonance. *Emotion is what will give your story power.* Make sure to give your story's character some kind of emotion. Think about the emotional response you're looking to get from the reader. Is it fear, survival, guilt, excitement, amusement, maybe even hope?

To get buy-in from your audience, you need to elicit emotion. What's the difference between your story and someone else's? What's the mission or purpose of your company? Why should your audience care?

YOUR STORY NEEDS TO BE CONSISTENT AND AUTHENTIC

It's not just what you say through your website or content but the entire experience your company has to offer based on your buyer persona's needs.

You can make any industry, any product, or any service stand out, and that's done with providing an experience.

YOU NEED TO KEEP THINGS CLEAR AND CONCISE

Everyone can benefit from cutting down a lengthy story. Ever had a friend tell you a story that took them 10 minutes to get through but probably could have taken less than a minute? Even long stories benefit when you whittle them down to just the most important parts.

And be specific. You're not trying to speak to everyone. *Your story and experience should not be a one-size-fits-all approach.* Communicating with the correct audience niche and creating that need is just as important, if not more important, than the story you're telling.

So remember: Create emotional appeal, be consistent and authentic, and keep the story clear and concise.

Before creating your story, plan who the character is, the tone of voice you'll be using, the conflict, and the resolution.

What Does a Good Story Look Like?

A lot of brands are creating great stories. Let's take a look at an example.

Wistia provides professional video hosting with amazing viewer analytics, HD video delivery, and marketing tools to help you understand your website visitors.

Wistia creates a whole bunch of fun and engaging educational videos. They also create other forms of content—blog posts, guides, help articles, and webinars.

Now, think back to the Golden Circle, starting with why.

Wistia's purpose is to empower everybody to get more out of video. Of course, their product helps with this, but it only solves a small percentage.

All of its content and storytelling circles back to this purpose.

Let's look at two pieces of content and see how Wistia did with their storytelling.

Wistia created the blog post shown in Figure 2.1: "Improve Your Audio: How to Reduce Echo in Your Video."

Right from the title, you can tell what the conflict is: reducing echo in your videos. A title isn't always going to be

FIGURE 2.1

FIGURE 2.2

about the conflict. Sometimes it might be the resolution, and other times it might summarize what the blog post is about, as in Figure 2.2.

But in this case, it's the conflict.

The blog post even starts out with "Bad sounding audio can ruin even the best of videos" (Figure 2.3). Their buyer persona can instantly relate. The audience is pulled into the conflict and is now likely asking for more.

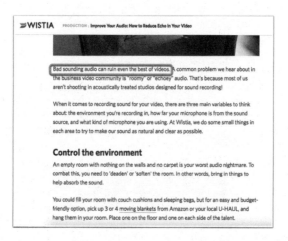

FIGURE 2.3

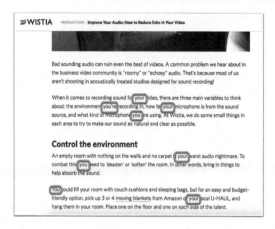

Figure 2.4

Let's dig deeper. Who's the character? Based on the title, it appears the character will be the audience or the reader because it's about improving "your" audio in "your" video.

As you can see, Wistia continues to use this point of view throughout the blog post (Figure 2.4).

And finally, the article provides the resolution—step-by-step instructions on soundproofing for video (Figure 2.5).

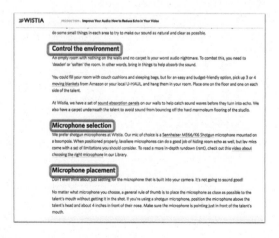

Figure 2.5

The story is clear and concise and ties back to Wistia's purpose: empowering people to get more out of video.

They use language and a funny tone to stay consistent and authentic with their brand. What's the difference between Wistia telling you this information and you finding a random video on YouTube?

Wistia does a good job of eliciting emotion and empathizing with their buyer persona. They make the conflict appear as something that needs to be resolved but isn't impossible to do. They teach while telling the story.

This is a simple piece of content, so how does this work for something that's more long form? You might find that for some of your content you'll be telling multiple stories in one.

Take this example: hiring an in-house video producer (Figure 2.6), which is another piece of content Wistia created. Like the earlier example, you can tell what the overall conflict is.

But the more you look at the content, the more you'll see there are several different conflicts that come up because there are several different stories.

Within this piece of content (Figure 2.7), all three points of views are used. Wistia talks about its own experience with this problem. Wista uses first person to relate to the audience, to let a reader know "Hey, we've been there, too!" As mentioned before, using first person is a way of being confessional.

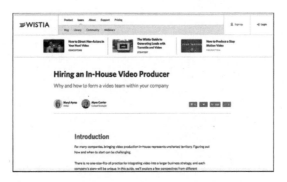

Figure 2.6

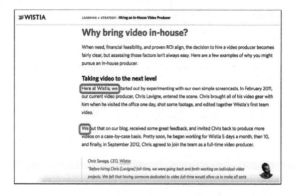

FIGURE 2.7

They use the second person (Figure 2.8) to describe next steps the reader can take to interview a video producer.

They even use case studies to help develop a third person point of view (Figure 2.9).

What's important to note is that within these smaller stories, Wistia is consistent with its point of view.

And as with all of its content, Wistia keeps the story clear and concise.

Wistia does a great job of storytelling, but now it's your turn. Use the Golden Circle, apply the three elements of a story, and always keep the best practices in mind.

FIGURE 2.8

FIGURE 2.9

Chapter 2 Homework

ACTIVITY 1

Wistia's purpose is to empower everybody to get more out of video.

Why does your company do what it does? In a Google Doc, write your business's why.

ACTIVITY 2

Regardless of the story you're trying to tell or how you're trying to tell it, storytelling has three essential elements: characters, conflict, and resolution.

In your Google Doc:

♦ Outline your business's character (the primary person you're trying to reach and educate or inform).
♦ Outline your business's conflict (the problem it's trying to solve).
♦ Outline your business's resolution (the solution it offers).

Chapter **3**

Generating Content Ideas

Why Do You Need a Process for Generating Content Ideas?

Humans are always coming up with new ideas. Whether we're lying in bed, commuting to work, or going for a run, our minds have a seemingly endless ability to generate new ideas.

But as natural and easy as this process may feel, it gets tricky when your job depends on it.

A content marketer—or any creative type, for that matter—doesn't have the leisure to have an "off day." *Your content ideas fuel your work.* Run out of gas, and your content initiatives will stall.

A content process helps you generate ideas that may not be easily apparent. Some ideas seem to drop from the heavens right into our minds, whereas others must be wrestled into submission. Those ideas are hard earned and not easily captured. You have to fight for them. The benefit is that it feels so much better when you finally unleash them into the world.

There are four main reasons why every content marketing professional needs to know how to generate content ideas:

Thank you to Guillaume Delloue for your contribution to this chapter.

1. Your days are busy.
2. You can uncover ideas that you may not have come up with on your own.
3. You will, at some point, run out of good ideas.
4. You need to keep up with increased demand of content creation.

Your Days Are Busy

You've got blog articles to write, webinars to record, and podcasts to produce. And not only do your content ideas need to be good, they must also be relevant to your buyer personas and align with your overall marketing strategy.

A content generation process will allow you to come up with a predictable flow of original, high-quality, and relevant content ideas.

A Content Generation Process Helps You Uncover Ideas That You May Not Have Come Up with on Your Own

No matter how inexhaustibly creative you are, you'd likely benefit from having other people help you brainstorm ideas.

Whether it's your colleagues, friends, family, or even your competition, you can benefit from the influence and perspectives of other people.

The Reality Is That Sooner or Later, You'll Run Out of Good Ideas

During the first few weeks or months on the job, ideas will come to you like bees to honey. Eventually content fatigue will set in, and you'll find yourself looking at the page with nothing to write.

You might be a creative, but you're also a professional. And one of the major differences between the professional writer and the amateur is that the former doesn't have the leisure to wait for inspiration to strike.

Think of a content generation process as your shield against writer's block.

CONTENT MARKETING AT SCALE REQUIRES PROVEN PROCESSES SO YOUR TEAM CAN GROW RESPONSIBLY AND KEEP UP WITH INCREASED DEMAND

For one, a process helps new hires ramp up quickly and start having an impact as quickly as possible, which also helps free up managers' time. And should your top talent leave or be unavailable, the rest of the team has a proven system to fall back on.

Where Do Ideas Come From?

Where do ideas come from? It's a bit of an odd question, isn't it? The ancient Greeks believed that actual goddesses—also known as muses—were responsible for our creative inspiration. In our day and age, content marketers and creative types need a little more. After all, you don't have the leisure to wait for the gods.

Instead, you might turn to famed advertising executive James Webb Young. In 1940, Young published the short book *A Technique for Producing Ideas*, which has become a favorite among copywriters and creative types of all stripes.[1]

Young's thesis is that idea creation isn't just about waiting for inspiration to strike—there's a process. And if you can understand that process, you can build a more efficient ideation process and become a better content marketer.

Young starts with the proposition that "an idea is nothing more nor less than a new combination of old elements" (p. 13).

That's why Hollywood producers will pitch a movie like *Jaws Meets Dinosaurs* or why entrepreneurs describe their startup as the "Uber for dog sitting"—all ideas are made up of different and often never previously connected elements in order to produce something new.

Now, Young's not the first person to have reached that conclusion—other creative types and scientists have said as much. What makes his perspective so interesting is how succinct his description of the ideation process is. He breaks it down into four steps:

1. Gather raw material.
2. Digest the material.
3. Use unconscious processing.
4. The eureka moment.

LET'S DIG DEEPER INTO EACH STEP, STARTING WITH GATHERING RAW MATERIAL Great content marketers read and consume content from a wide variety of places. They're endlessly curious and fascinated by a wide breadth of topics. All these things make up the "raw material"—all the facts, concepts, and stories that float in your mind in a sort of suspended animation.

So, be curious. Read whatever you can, whenever you can. Develop an appetite for content and consume it regularly—good, bad, old, new, popular, niche. Not just marketing content, either. Consume history, poetry, or science magazines on top of Snapchat stories and industry blogs. Let it all seep into your mind. You might be surprised what will come of it.

It also helps to maintain a repository for all those ideas. The old school term is "swipe file," which is an actual folder where people kept newspaper clippings and other bits of content. But in the digital era, this could be tools like Google Docs, Evernote, bookmarks, or whatever other platform works best for you.

IN THE SECOND STAGE, YOU'LL DIGEST THE MATERIAL
The goal is to bring those disparate ideas together and see how they fit. You're looking for relationships, connections, and

combinations. The goal is to synthesize those ideas in interesting and compelling ways.

Think of this stage as content digestion. You want to turn those ideas upside down and consider them from all possible angles.

IN THE THIRD STAGE, YOU'LL USE UNCONSCIOUS PROCESSING

Stop trying to bring those ideas together and do something else entirely—listen to music, go out for a run, or watch a movie—anything to take your mind off the process. Let your unconscious take over. Sometimes you have to let your mind rest and organize itself on its own. Even when you're not actively thinking about a problem, the mind has its own way of processing information and making connections. Use it.

AND THEN COMES THE FOURTH AND FINAL STAGE— THE EUREKA MOMENT

Suddenly, and seemingly out of nowhere, an idea will pop into your head. As Young says, "It will come to you when you are least expecting it." You might be brushing your teeth or simply walking to work, and a fully formed idea will arrive unexpectedly. When that happens, make sure to document it. Millions of ideas have been lost by people who thought they would remember them.

This process isn't anything new or terribly surprising. It's how all of us come up with ideas. But as creative types, it's valuable to be aware of each step so you can work on them and improve.

It's especially important to spend time gathering the raw material. Curiosity and the will to act on it is a helpful prerequisite for any content marketer. You have to be willing and able to read voraciously and consume content from all places, not just from your industry.

Now that we've looked at how ideas are formed, let's look at some specific ways to generate ideas for your content marketing efforts.

How Do You Generate Ideas for Content Creation?

Okay, so now that you understand the process of ideation, let's dig into a few ways you can generate ideas to help fuel your content marketing efforts.

There are two different ways you can generate content ideas:

1. By yourself
2. With a group

Experiment with both, and soon you'll come up with a process that makes sense for your specific needs.

Let's Start with Creating Ideas on Your Own

There are four things you should keep in mind when generating content ideas on your own, including:

1. What are your buyer persona's reading habits?
2. What are your competitors doing?
3. What are people talking about on discussion websites like Quora?
4. What can you learn from your search engine optimization efforts?

Let's take a look.

First, What Are Your Buyer Persona's Reading Habits?

Put yourself in the shoes of your prospects. Empathize with them. What are their challenges and pain points? What do they read on the web and get educated about? Is there a specific blog or website they frequently visit?

If you can, try interviewing some of your best customers by phone or email and find out about their reading habits. You can even include a question on your form that explores visitors' go-to outlets.

Once you have a list of websites or blogs, use a tool like Buzzsumo to see which content has the best social media performance.[2]

Just type a domain name, and you'll get a list of the associated pages along with their performance by social media channel.

For example, let's imagine you're writing for a Boston-based real estate company. Type "Boston real estate" in Buzzsumo and check out the top results.

You'll find posts about how much it costs to live near Boston's MBTA stops, what rising real estate prices mean for the area, and what you need to earn on average in order to afford a typical apartment. From just a simple search, you can get a sense of the most talked-about social media posts about Boston real estate and get plenty of topic ideas to fuel your content marketing.

Alternatively, you can go directly to various blogs—ones that you know are favorites within your industry—and look at the most popular posts. Look for blog posts that receive the most social and comment engagement.

Next, what are your competitors doing?   Another tactic that is especially helpful if you're unsure about your persona's reading habits is to look at your competitors' content marketing efforts. If you share a similar target audience, it's likely the content that performs well on their sites will also appeal to your prospects. So look at what they're producing and what's really resonating. Here again, use Buzzsumo to quickly scan their websites and see what's performing well.

Next, what are people talking about on discussion forums?   What is your audience talking about on Quora, a popular question-and-answer site where anyone can ask a question and get answers from the community?[3]

Although anyone can participate, moderators do a great job of limiting noise and keeping quality high.

Sometimes you might not be able to find out where your audience lives online. That's okay. Another approach to coming up with content generation ideas is to start with a set of keywords related to your industry or profession.

For example, let's assume your target audience is business development representatives.

After searching for "business development representatives," Quora will return a series of popular questions that contain the keyword, such as "What are some good and bad practices on compensating business development representatives?" Without even looking at the answers, this tactic provides valuable insights into common challenges and questions for individuals in that field.

Lastly, what can you learn from your search engine optimization efforts?   There are a few search engine optimization tools and techniques you can use to generate content ideas. A go-to is the Google Search Console (formerly known as Google Webmaster Tools).[4] Assuming it's properly verified with your domain, you should be able to view sample queries users typed into Google to find your website as well as topics you're looking for, even if it's not on the first page. This is valuable data because you're getting actual keywords people are typing in.

Here are three other quick ways to make the most of Google. Use:

1. Autocomplete functionality
2. Related searches
3. Specific keywords and topics that rank on the first search engine results page (SERP)

Autocomplete happens when Google suggests a query as you type in the search bar.   These "search predictions" might uncover ideas around a topic that you hadn't thought about.

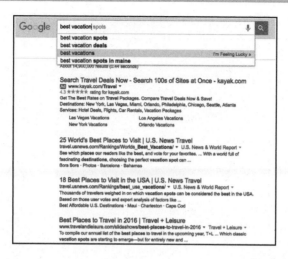

FIGURE 3.1

Let's assume you're looking for content ideas about vacations. Type in "best vacation," and Google will auto-complete with "best vacation spots" or "best vacation deals" (see Figure 3.1).

Related searches appear at the bottom of the search results page and offer additional suggestions. (see Figure 3.2). For example, let's assume you type into Google "Is cat litter toxic?" Google's related searches will suggest "Is cat litter toxic to humans?" or even "Is cat litter biodegradable?"

And lastly, perform a series of searches based on keywords or topics your buyer persona might use. You can learn a lot from the content that ranks on the first page of Google.

For example, if you performed a search query for "2017 digital marketing trends," you'd receive the SERP shown in Figure 3.3.

Take the time to click through and review various listings on the SERP that catch your eye. I recommend digging deeper into the top five search results first, because that's where the

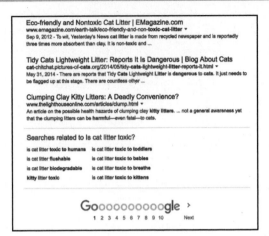

majority of people click; the first two positions account for 51% of search traffic.[5]

When clicking through to each listing, look for three things:

1. **How in-depth is the content?** Is there an opportunity to expand on a specific point or the entire content as a whole?

2. **Is it current?** Is there new industry information that can bring value to the content?

3. **Is the user experience positive?** Is there an opportunity to create something that is more user-friendly? Is there anything you can learn from the content that you can use to optimize your user experience?

Let's take a look at the fourth listing in Figure 3.3: "7 Digital Marketing Trends That Will Rule 2017 [INFOGRAPHIC]." We know right out of the gate that this is going to be a visual resource based on the listing including the word infographic in its title.

The listing is for a company called Venngage, which offers a tool that helps you tell stories and present your data with infographics.[6] Their resource is a great example of content that's in-depth, up to date, and offers a high-quality user experience.

To start, Venngage created an infographic to tell their story in a visual manner (see Figure 3.4)—a smart and effective way to help people consume and remember content; 90% of information transmitted to the brain is visual.[7] But they didn't stop there. They allow you to take the infographic with you by offering the source code needed to embed it on your website. What a clever way to share a resource.

Moving down the page, Venngage offers a descriptive section with either a data point or example(s) to supplement and support each trend's claim from the infographic (see Figure 3.5).

But do you see anything that can be improved? Somewhere you might be able to provide more unique value? The content for each trend mentioned is short and concise. Maybe there's an opportunity to dig deeper into a specific concept with prescriptive tactics or strategies.

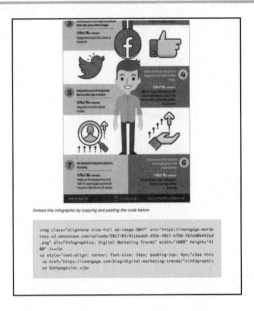

FIGURE 3.4

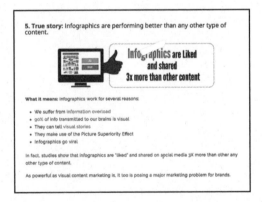

FIGURE 3.5

Lastly, don't stop after reviewing one listing. There's a SERP with nine other listings just waiting for you to read them. If you see something you like or that gets your creative juices flowing, document it. Don't expect to remember it later.

You could host a company brainstorm. A brainstorm can be a productive way to generate fresh and creative content ideas. By inviting team members who don't spend their day thinking about content, you'll likely get new ideas from a different perspective.

There are hundreds of ways to format and host a brainstorm. To help you get started, here's a list of best practices when hosting a brainstorm:

1. Select someone to moderate and set a clear agenda.
2. Create an atmosphere where people feel comfortable.
3. Use "braindumps."
4. Use sticky notes, whiteboards, and other visual aids.
5. Remember that the main goal is to generate new, unexpected ideas.

First, select someone to moderate the meeting and set a clear agenda. Agenda items could include different topics or questions: What's the problem we're trying to solve? How long will the session last? And what are the rules of engagement? However, brainstorms can quickly dissolve into an unproductive group hangout if there's no direction. Make sure someone owns the meeting and that everyone follows his or her guidelines.

Next, create an atmosphere where people feel comfortable sharing their ideas. It can be uncomfortable to ask coworkers to come up with random ideas, especially the people who aren't used to doing so on a regular basis. People get self-conscious, so use icebreakers.

For example, run through a basic word-association game. The first person says a word, let's use "fries," then the following person mentions another association, like "French" or "cheese," and on and on until either the first word is mentioned again or a certain amount of time has elapsed. It's amazing what connections people make. This is a great way to get your creative juices flowing.

Next, use braindumps. A braindump is an uninterrupted period of time (typically no more than two to three minutes long) when you jot down all the ideas that come to your mind. The goal is quantity, not quality. Don't overthink your answers or wonder how good they are. Just get them on paper as quickly as possible.

For example, if you are writing content for a pool company, you could suggest a braindump about all the topics that come to mind when you think about pool types, styles, and maintenance. Suggestions might include "Fiberglass vs. concrete pools: Which is better?" or "Pool caring tips you need to know." *This type of exercise works equally well with experts and people who don't know anything about the topic.*

Also, use sticky notes, whiteboards, and other visual aids to keep track of ideas. Sticky notes are especially effective, because it's easy to group them together by topic and identify trends and common themes. Try to display everyone's ideas so the process feels democratic and transparent. You want the experience to be positive so people will want to do it again in the future.

Constraints breed creativity. So make sure to set strict time limits—both for the length of the meeting (no longer than an hour) and the braindumps. You can sometimes let people voice good ideas after the time is up, but make sure they're exceptions.

Finally, remember that the main goal of a brainstorm is to generate new, unexpected ideas. It might not be the time to refine those ideas or critique them. So if all you get out of these sessions is a dozen or so ideas to expand and improve upon, that might be enough.

And there you have it. Now you have a process to help you generate content ideas.

Chapter 3 Homework

ACTIVITY 1

It's important to document your thoughts when inspiration strikes. Open a new Google Sheet and create a digital swipe file to store your ideas.

Figure 3.6 is a sample digital swipe file to help you get started. Follow this link to access the template: bit.ly/2f9xPNq.

Pro tip: Have Google Drive accessible on your mobile device and set it to use files offline. This way, you can document ideas on the go and have them upload to the cloud once cell reception is available.

ACTIVITY 2

Perform a search query for a topic or keyword your audience would use to find content relevant to your business or industry. Click on one of the top search results.

Consider the three things we looked for when we clicked through to Venngage's page, "2017 digital marketing trends":

1. **How in-depth is the content?** Is there an opportunity to expand on a specific point or the entire content as a whole?
2. **Is it current?** Is there new industry information that can bring value to the content?

URL / Title	What I like about it?	Notes
https://venngage.com/blog/digital-marketing-trends/	Includes infographic source code to embed on website; Offers supplemental examples and data to support infographic claims	Opportunity to expand on various trends with specific tactics and strategies

FIGURE **3.6**

3. **Is the user experience positive?** Is there an opportunity to create something that's more user-friendly? Is there anything you can learn from the content that you can use to optimize your user experience?

In your digital swipe file, write down:

◆ What's the title of the page you clicked on?
◆ What's something unique or interesting about the content that you like? Does it provide a positive reading experience?
◆ Are there any areas of opportunity in this search for you to provide unique, interesting thought leadership value? If so, what are they?

ACTIVITY 3

Make a list of three ideas for your next blog post. Each idea should be educational or informative about your industry, not about your brand. Most people don't know who you are yet, so you need to attract them with valuable thought leadership content.

After you generate ideas for your next blog posts, write down what you learned from this idea-generation exercise. Were there any specific techniques you found helpful?

Chapter 4

Planning a Long-Term Content Strategy

Why Long-Term Content Planning Is Important

Planning provides a road map for your content. You wouldn't get in a car and drive without an end destination; you'd be wasting gas. This is probably why 86% of highly effective organizations have someone steering the direction of their content strategy.[1]

At this point, you know how important content is to your content marketing strategy, but it's important to remember that content has the important job of pulling people from one stage of the inbound methodology to another (see Figure 4.1).

It plays an integral part in each and every stage of the buyer's journey.

When it Comes to Creating Content, You Want to Remain as Reactive and Agile as You Can to Make the Most of Your Time

Having a plan will give you and your team the ability to remain reactive to upcoming initiatives, to stay organized, and to proactively manage content required for your marketing tasks.

Think of your long-term content strategy like a savings account. If your goal is to retire someday, you need a plan,

Thank you to Joseph Del Bene for your contribution to this chapter.

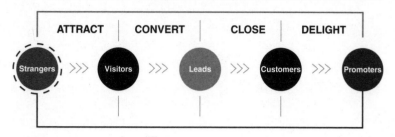

FIGURE 4.1

and you need to be consistent with your contributions. The more consistent you are, and the better you are with your contributions, the bigger your return on investment (ROI) will be. But in order to retire, you need to be consistent month after month; otherwise, you'll miss your goals and the ability to retire.

The same can be said about your content. If you make a plan and you're consistent in your approach, you're giving yourself the best chance at achieving ROI from your content efforts. You'll have the opportunity to grow an expansive library of content, making you and your business content-wealthy.

It's important to note that obstacles and roadblocks will come up along the way, but at least you have your goals and direction set. Having a plan will make it that much easier to regain alignment as well as understand bandwidth and priorities for what needs to get done and when.

ANOTHER REASON THAT YOU SHOULD HAVE A LONG-TERM CONTENT STRATEGY IS IT HELPS YOU STAY ORGANIZED

Most often, marketing teams place a focus on more than one initiative at any given time. A long-term plan accounts for all upcoming initiatives and provides the ability to be agile in your content creation process.

Being organized will also help you align your content marketing goals with the overall goals of the business. In essence, it gets the marketing team in line with the current initiatives of the entire organization.

Content is not just about supporting the marketing team; it should be about supporting the sales team, customer service team, product and services teams, and so on.

By aligning your content marketing goals to the overall goals of the organization, you can rest assured that your focus will provide an immediate impact where it matters most, attracting and attaining the attention of your audience.

Lastly, Long-term Planning Helps you Tell a Story by Taking Your Audience Through the Buyer's Journey

Remember, content is the fuel that keeps the inbound methodology running. Having a relevant content approach like this gives you the opportunity to answer your prospects' questions and meet them at their point of need.

How Do You Build a Long-Term Content Strategy?

Let's take a moment to revisit the buyer's journey and review how it relates to the marketing funnel. When you put these two together we like to call it the "marketing machine." The marketing machine relates each buyer's journey stage to a corresponding marketing funnel stage:

- ◆ The awareness stage relates to visits and leads.
- ◆ The consideration stage relates to marketing qualified leads, or MQLs, and sales qualified leads, or SQLs.
- ◆ The decision stage relates to opportunities and customers.

These funnels are designed to help you visualize and guide a prospect through the stages of the buyer's journey so that you can effectively measure your funnel and provide a tailored message to that prospect during their particular stage of the buyer's journey.

It's important to understand the relationship between both funnels because they're working toward the same goals: attracting your prospects, converting them into leads, and closing them into customers.

A marketing machine is not developed overnight. It takes a lot of time and planning to build. This is where a long-term content strategy comes in. So what's involved in developing a long-term content strategy?

There are three steps you must take to create a long-term content strategy:

1. Set your marketing goals.
2. Audit or assess your organization's initiatives and assets.
3. Understand the buyer's journey for your buyer personas.

The ultimate objective here is to have a unifying document you can use to keep track of your long-term content marketing initiatives.

First, Let's Talk About Setting Your Marketing Goals

Setting marketing goals provides you with long-term vision and short-term motivation. It helps you organize your time and resources so you can make the most of your content creation efforts.

Each piece of content created for a marketing initiative should be tied to a goal that's also directly related to the overarching goals of the organization. This will help you stay laser-focused during the content creation process.

Let's take a second to think about this. If your company's quarterly customer goal is 15 new customers, and you know the number of leads needed to generate 15 customers is 50 leads, and if you know the number of website visits needed to generate 50 leads is 1,000 visits, then you need to take into consideration the content needed to hit your visits goal.

Each goal you set should be a SMART goal. That is, it should be:

Specific

Measurable

Attainable

Relevant

Timely

A potential SMART goal could be: "Increase quarterly site visits by 20%. That's 5,000 to 6,000 per quarter by the end of the year."

Auditing or Assessing Your Organization's Initiatives and Assets Is the Second Step in Creating a Long-Term Content Strategy

Your audit will consist of two parts:

1. Auditing your content assets
2. Auditing your event-based priorities

Let's begin with the content audit. Your goal with the content audit is to identify all the marketing assets you have at your disposal and potential gaps or opportunities in your content strategy.

For every marketer who has been generating content for a while, there comes a point when they realize they have no idea where all their content is or how much they actually have.

You, your predecessors, or other individuals in the marketing department, often including subject matter experts from other departments, have likely created content, and it is scattered just about everywhere.

By doing your content audit, you'll be able to identify resources that you already have, which could save you hours of content creation time in the future. There's no use in duplicating your efforts.

When it comes to documenting a content audit, there should be a place for you to insert all your assets and properly categorize them based on:

♦ Content title
♦ Buyer's journey stage
♦ Marketing funnel stage
♦ Format or type of content
♦ Which buyer persona it's targeting
♦ Topic
♦ Any additional notes that provide value or context

Now it's time to do some digging for content assets, such as guides, worksheets, or sales collateral. Start by systematically combing through the dark corners where content can typically hide, like that old file manager or marketing folder on your computer. Ask your sales team what type of collateral they use. Check in with the more tenured employees (you'll be surprised at the wealth of knowledge here). Pore through your customer relationship management system (CRM) and your content management system (CMS).

Okay, I think you get the picture here. Let's take a look at a content audit from a HubSpot customer by the name of Maren Schmidt (Figure 4.2). Maren offers advice and resources backed by over 30 years of experience working with young children.

Content Audit Worksheet						
Content Title	**Buyer's Journey Stage**	**Marketing Funnel Stage (Lifecycle Stage)**	**Format/Type**	**Buyer Persona**	**Topic**	**Notes**
Type The Title of the Content Offer Here	Map the piece of content to the relevant Buyer's Journey stage (Awareness, Consideration, or Decision)	Map the content to your specific stage of the marketing funnel (Subscriber, Lead, Marketing Qualified Lead, Opportunity, Customer)	Identify the content type/format	Select the Buyer Persona(s)	Identify the topic covered in this piece of content	If needed, provide context for content
7 Parenting Problems you can avoid	Awareness	Lead	ebook	Montessori Mom Meena	Parenting Problems	7 Tips parents can use to help avoid common bad habbit's children develop
Understanding Montessori: A Guide For Parents	Consideration	Lead	Study guide	Montessori Mom Meena	Understanding montessori and it's benefits	
Steps to Reading Success	Decision	MQL	Webinar	Montessori Mom Meena Montessori Teacher Tammy Head of School Heidi	A preview of our workshop on reading success	
Understanding Montessori Newsletter Series	Awareness	Lead	Newsletter Series	Montessori Mom Meena Montessori Teacher Tammy Head of School Heidi	For parents and teachers who are interested in an emphasis on teaching and learning the Montessori way.	
Finding Motivation the Montessori Way	Decision	MQL	Workshop Video Introduction	Montessori Teacher Tammy Head of School Heidi	Ever wish you could explain how and why Montessori students develop internal motivation and self-discipline?	
Montessori Professional Development Workshop Preview	Decision	MQL	Workshop Video Introduction	Montessori Teacher Tammy Head of School Heidi	School leaders looking for fresh ways to help your staff get the professional development they need and deserve	

FIGURE 4.2

Notice how Maren already has content spanning the Awareness, Consideration, and Decision stages of the buyer's journey for multiple buyer personas, and each piece of content corresponds to a specific lifecycle stage. Additionally, Maren has many different types of content formats to offer her buyer personas, such as an ebook, a study guide, and a webinar. Notice how Maren uses the Notes field to explain the contents of her content offer, though she may not need this for each piece of content in her audit.

Now that Maren has documented her assets, she'll be able to refer to this audit in the future to help pinpoint what content she already has and how it can help with future content creation initiatives.

The second part of completing your audit is to conduct an audit of your event-based initiatives. What I mean by this is you'll need to take into account any upcoming projects, priorities, or events that would involve content creation.

Doing this exercise will help you identify content that could support each initiative as well as give you an opportunity to see how you can connect this content back to the buyer's journey through an inbound marketing campaign.

An event-based audit should be organized by the following areas:

- ◆ Upcoming priorities by month
- ◆ Initiative overview
- ◆ Theme
- ◆ Prospective blog post topics that support an inbound marketing campaign

Take a look at what Maren did for her event-based audit (Figure 4.3).

You can see that Maren has a few events and workshops that she may need content for. You can also see that the content

Event-Based Audit Worksheet				
Month	Webinar / Event / Seasonal Change / Company Priority / Holiday	Themes	Keywords / Blog Post Topics	Inbound Marketing Campaigns (Marketing Machine / Buyer's Journey Funnel)
January	Paid Workshops: Seeing Your Child the Montessori Way Webinar: Preparing your home the montessori way		Montessori Professional Development	
February	Paid Workshops: Reading Fundamentals Event: Montessori Professional Development Workshop	Montessori For Parents, Teachers, and Principals	How to talk to teachers about Montessori	ebook: Preparing Your Home the Montessori Way
March	Live Q&A		Helping Parents "Get Montessori"	

FIGURE 4.3

is grouped into an overall theme for the next three months with associated blog topics that integrate with an inbound marketing campaign called "Preparing Your Home the Montessori Way," which is an ebook.

Try to imagine for a minute if Maren only planned the month, initiative overview, and theme without keywords and blog post topics that associate with a relevant inbound marketing campaign.

Yes, she would have noted that there are a number of events coming up in the next few months, but she would have missed out on the opportunity to tie everything together with a series of predetermined blog posts that could lead to a relevant content offer that would provide value to her marketing machine. Simply adding these two columns helps maximize your content potential and forces you to think bigger than just the events at hand.

The Last Important Step to Create a Sustainable Long–Term Content Strategy Is Understanding the Buyer's Journey for Your Buyer Personas

Remember, you're creating content that's meant to attract and pull your buyer personas through every stage of the buyer's journey—from the Awareness stage, where it's more problem-based, through the Consideration stage, where you're discussing a solution, and ending in the Decision stage, where you're recommending next steps (i.e., helpful product or service). Simply identifying this content will help you generate content ideas to work with in the future.

But before you can understand the buyer's journey, you first need to know your buyer personas.

Keeping this in mind, let's take a look at one of Maren's buyer personas, Montessori Mom Meena.

Meena's a devoted mother, working professional, and married with at least one child under the age of six.

Meena wants to understand child development and do what's best for her children, understand how to set limits for behavior, and have effective communication tools to use with her children.

Meena's challenges are her children's refusal to listen and she has to deal with tantrums, all of which overwhelm her as a parent.

Maren knows that Meena uses Google to find answers to problems she's looking to solve.

Now that you know who Meena is, let's take a look at what the buyer's journey might look like for her in more detail (see Figure 4.4).

To start, you know it's important for Meena to do what's best for her children, so what about an awareness-stage ebook that lists parenting problems you can avoid? This is something that would bring value to Meena's search.

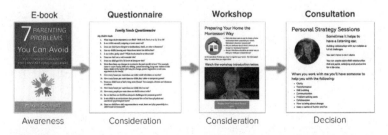

FIGURE 4.4

Then, once Meena's been educated on parenting problems to avoid, what about following up with Consideration-stage information, like a questionnaire about family needs to help her understand a possible solution—in this case, Montessori? The questionnaire outlines both the needs of the child and the parent.

But maybe Meena needs a little more information to help pull her toward the Decision stage, something that educates her on how to best prepare for Montessori. What about a free Consideration-stage workshop that explains how to prepare your home the Montessori way? That could do the trick.

And now that Meena has found a solution to her problem in Montessori, she can make a well-informed, confident decision. What about offering Meena a one-hour strategy consultation to discuss next steps for her child and Montessori? Sounds about right.

That's an example of a complete buyer's journey.

It's important to note that a buyer's journey is ever evolving. The more you learn about your buyer personas, the more you'll be able to understand and speak to them over time. But this starts with first identifying content needed to complete the buyer's journey, which you can then plan out over the course of a year to keep your content creation sustainable.

What a Long-Term Content Strategy Should Look Like

Now that you've completed your audits and identified content opportunities for your buyer personas, it's time to organize them with your content compass.

Why a compass?

Well, a compass is an instrument for determining directions. Simply put, a content compass is a worksheet that helps you organize the direction of your content creation.

Your content compass needs to have the following attributes. It needs to be in real time, which will circumvent

FIGURE 4.5

version-control issues with previous edits. It needs to allow multiple contributors access to collaborate. Let's take a look at how Maren built it using a Google Sheet.

Maren started filling in and organizing her content compass from the audits she performed and the buyer's journey content she identified (Figure 4.5).

As you can see, the content compass organizes the direction of content and priorities by theme and connects them to a specific month, which descends down the sheet.

First, you can see that Maren has listed her SMART goals for January, February, and March. Notice how each goal is clearly defined and measureable: "complete 75% of enrollment for workshops."

Next, you can see Maren has a theme she's going to focus on for January, February, and March: Montessori for parents, teachers, and principals. Keep in mind, you don't need a theme to extend for an entire quarter. You could have a theme for each month based on initiatives and the direction of your business.

Next, you can see that Maren has made a list of keywords and blog post topics that she plans to focus on, which tie into her overall theme.

Next (Figure 4.6), Maren has identified an inbound marketing campaign that's both relevant to the overall theme and brings value to her buyer persona. Also, notice how the blog posts directly correlate with the inbound marketing campaign, an opportunity where Maren could recycle blog post content

Content Compass							
Month	**Inbound Marketing Campaign(s)**	**Workshop(s)**	**External Event(s)**	**Webinar(s)**	**Email(s)**	**Facebook**	**Twitter**
January		Paid Workshops: Seeing Your Child the Montessori Way		Preparing your home the Montessori Way Webinar	Kids Talk Newsletter; weekly expert advice email; email for blogs; email series promoting workshop; email series promoting webinar; email promoting ebook	Posts supporting blogs; posts supporting workshops; posts supporting webinar; posts supporting ebook	Tweets supporting blogs; tweets supporting workshops; tweets supporting webinar; tweets supporting ebook
February	ebook: Preparing Your Home the Montessori Way	Paid Workshops: Reading Fundamentals	Montessori Professional Development Conference		Education Professional Newsletter; weekly expert advice email; email for blogs; email series promoting workshop; email series promoting external event; email promoting ebook	Posts supporting blogs; posts supporting workshops; posts supporting external event; posts supporting ebook	Tweet supporting blogs; tweets supporting workshops; tweets supporting external event; tweets supporting ebook
March		Live Q&A			Montessori Newsletter; weekly expert advice email; email for blogs; email series promoting Live Q&A; email promoting ebook	Posts supporting blogs; posts supporting Live Q&A; posts supporting ebook	Tweets supporting blogs; tweets supporting Live Q&A; tweets supporting ebook

FIGURE 4.6

into her content offer, saving her even more time and making her a more efficient content marketer.

Next, there's a series of workshops every month and a conference and webinar in February. Again, it's important to account for these initiatives in case content needs to arise to support them outside of inbound specific initiatives.

Next, you'll see email communication. Email communication is twofold. There are the regularly occurring emails like Maren's weekly advice, and there's also an email series promoting each of the month's initiatives, whether it is a webinar, external event, or workshop (Figure 4.7).

Next, you'll see all social media communication broken down by channel. Figure 4.7 shows that Maren focuses on Facebook, Twitter, and LinkedIn. Just like email, each channel focuses on promoting the month's initiatives.

Next, you'll see that Maren has a sales-focused campaign in January. Although she may not be sure now if she'll need content for this campaign, she has it documented so it's on her radar.

Content Compass							
Month	**Webinar(s)**	**Email(s)**	**Facebook**	**Twitter**	**LinkedIn**	**Sales Campaign(s)**	**Other**
January	Preparing your home the Montessori Way Webinar	Kids Talk Newsletter; weekly expert advice email; email for blogs; email series promoting workshop; email series promoting webinar; email promoting ebook	Posts supporting blogs; posts supporting workshops; posts supporting ebook	Tweets supporting blogs; tweets supporting workshops; tweets supporting webinar; tweets supporting ebook	Posts supporting blogs; posts supporting workshops; posts supporting ebook	Head of Montessori Schools Call Campaign	
February		Education Professional Newsletter; weekly expert advice email; email for blogs; email series promoting workshop; email promoting external event; email promoting ebook	Posts supporting blogs; posts supporting workshops; posts supporting external event; posts supporting ebook	Tweet supporting blogs; tweets supporting workshops; tweets supporting external event; tweets supporting ebook	Posts supporting blogs; posts supporting workshops; posts supporting external event; posts supporting ebook		
March		Montessori Newsletter; weekly expert advice email; email for blogs; email promoting ebook	Posts supporting blogs; posts supporting Live Q&A; posts supporting ebook	Tweets supporting blogs; tweets supporting Live Q&A; tweets supporting ebook	Posts supporting blogs; posts supporting Live Q&A; posts supporting ebook		

FIGURE 4.7

And finally, you'll see there's an "Other" column. You never know when something will come up that doesn't fall under one of the designated columns. In the ever-changing digital media space, there's always a new opportunity, a new platform, or a new test that you may want to perform. This column is reserved for new developments, such as republishing blog content on LinkedIn or performing a paid retargeting test on Facebook to increase workshop enrollment.

This is what your content organization should look like—each column connecting to the next. This way, you're ensuring your message is conveyed across multiple platforms. If you don't do this, all your communication channels might look disconnected, and that won't get you anywhere.

The next step for Maren is to wash, rinse, and repeat this process for the entire year. It takes a lot of thought and effort to create a long-term plan. If you're having trouble, break it up into quarters, just as Maren did. Getting frustrated and eager to start creating content without a plan will only hurt your results in the future.

And that's it. Use this information to not only help you create a long-term content strategy but also organize your yearly efforts in pursuit of those SMART goals.

Chapter 4 Homework

ACTIVITY 1
Create a SMART goal for the next content offer you plan to create. (Sample SMART goal: Increase quarterly site visits by 20%.) *Document in your Google Drive.*

ACTIVITY 2
What content has your business already produced? Let's find out by performing a content audit.

1. Open a new Google Sheet and name it "Content Planning Materials."
2. Rename the first tab "Content audit."

Figure 4.8 is an outline of the content audit Maren Schmidt performed. Follow this link to access the template: bit.ly/2gPTZrE.

Activity 3

Does your business have any upcoming events? Let's document them by performing an event-based audit.

♦ Open your Google Sheet titled "Content Planning Material."
♦ Create a new tab and rename it "Event-based audit."

Figure 4.9 is an outline of the event-based audit Maren Schmidt performed. Follow this link to access the template: bit.ly/2gPTZrE.

Activity 4

Schedule a team meeting, invite team members from different departments who work with your prospects and customers (sales,

Content Audit Worksheet						
Content Title	Buyer's Journey Stage	Marketing Funnel Stage (Lifecycle Stage)	Format/Type	Buyer Persona	Topic	Notes
Type The Title of the Content Offer Here	Map the piece of content to the relevant Buyer's Journey stage (Awareness, Consideration, or Decision)	Map the content to your specific stage of the marketing funnel (Subscriber, Lead, Marketing Qualified Lead, Opportunity, Customer)	Identify the content type/format	Select the Buyer Persona(s)	Identify the topic covered in this piece of content	If needed, provide context for content
7 Parenting Problems you can avoid	Awareness	Lead	ebook	Montessori Mom Meena	Parenting Problems	7 Tips parents can use to help avoid common bad habbit's children develop
Understanding Montessori A Guide For Parents	Consideration	Lead	Study guide	Montessori Mom Meena	Understanding montessori and it's benefits	
Steps to Reading Success	Decision	MQL	Webinar	Montessori Mom Meena Montessori Teacher Tammy Head of School Heidi	A preview of our workshop on reading success	
Understanding Montessori Newsletter Series	Awareness	Lead	Newsletter Series	Montessori Mom Meena Montessori Teacher Tammy Head of School Heidi	For parents and teachers who are interested in an emphasis on teaching and learning the Montessori way.	
Finding Motivation the Montessori Way	Decision	MQL	Workshop Video Introduction	Montessori Teacher Tammy Head of School Heidi	Ever wish you could explain how and why Montessori students develop internal motivation and self-discipline?	
Montessori Professional Development Workshop Preview	Decision	MQL	Workshop Video Introduction	Montessori Teacher Tammy Head of School Heidi	School leaders looking for fresh ways to help your staff get the professional development they need and deserve	

Figure 4.8

Event-Based Audit Worksheet				
Month	**Webinar / Event / Seasonal Change / Company Priority / Holiday**	**Themes**	**Keywords / Blog Post Topics**	**Inbound Marketing Campaigns (Marketing Machine / Buyer's Journey Funnel)**
January	Paid Workshops: Seeing Your Child the Montessori Way Webinar: Preparing your home the montessori way		Montessori Professional Development	
February	Paid Workshops: Reading Fundamentals Event: Montessori Professional Development Workshop	Montessori For Parents, Teachers, and Principals	How to talk to teachers about Montessori	ebook: Preparing Your Home the Montessori Way
March	Live Q&A		Helping Parents "Get Montessori"	

FIGURE 4.9

marketing, support, etc.), and create a detailed buyer persona for your business using this link: http://www.makemypersona.com.

It's important to include other team members from various departments for two reasons:

1. You'll paint the best picture of your audience by having input from multiple team members from different departments.

2. Including others from different teams helps break down the departments' barrier walls, making it possible to get buy-in on content marketing as a business-wide initiative.

ACTIVITY 5

Identify the buyer's journey for your buyer persona. The goal is to help them through the Awareness, Consideration, and Decision stages. And while there's no magic number for the amount of content in the buyer's journey, let's start off with identifying three pieces of content—one for each stage of the buyer's journey.

We recommend starting with a comprehensive, educational awareness-stage resource like a guide or ebook. This way, you can prove your subject matter expertise and help educate your buyer persona about your industry, which is a great way to start building a valuable relationship.

Write out the following:

1. Awareness stage
   • Resource type (e.g., ebook, guide)
   • Theme (what do you want to communicate?)
2. Consideration stage
   • Resource type (e.g., checklist, case study)
   • Theme (what do you want to communicate?)
3. Decision stage
   • Resource type (e.g., consultation, demo)
   • Theme (what do you want to communicate?)

ACTIVITY 6

Create an outline for your long-term content strategy by creating a content compass.

1. Open your Google Sheet titled "Content Planning Material."
2. Create a new tab and rename it "Content compass."
3. Organize the buyer's journey content you identified for your primary buyer persona by monthly inbound marketing campaigns.

Figure 4.10 is a sample of the content compass Maren Schmidt identified. Follow this link to access the template: bit.ly/2gPTZrE.

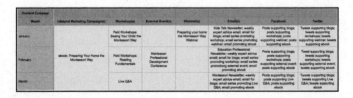

FIGURE 4.10

Chapter **5**

Becoming an Effective Writer

Why Effective Writing Matters

Let me start by telling you a little secret: *Even for professional writers, writing is hard.* It's not a skill that's learned naturally.

But words are the currency of the web. And to be an effective marketer, you need to learn to use these words in ways that benefit your business and brand.

So why does effective writing matter so much?

At its core, effective content is relevant and useful to your audience—your reader. It makes your reader, not your company and its revenue targets or goals, your number one priority. Your writing should use your audience's language and show that you understand their pain points, challenges, and goals. It should be produced to help people, not just sell them on your products or services.

On average, people consume 285 pieces of content, or 54,000 words, every single day.[1]

That's a lot of words competing for one person's attention.

Your writing must slow down the reader and prevent them from clicking another link. It has to get them to stop, read, think, learn, and consider what you have to say.

Thank you to Jami Oetting for your contribution to this chapter.

To get your audience to put on the brakes as they browse, *your writing has to be helpful and useful*. And when your content is helpful and useful, day after day, month after month, people begin to connect with you and your business. They begin to trust your ideas and knowledge because of how you've expressed them and what they've learned from you. And then they begin to rely on you as a source of information.

This is a great position to be in with your prospects—you've developed a relationship that leaves them wanting more information from you.

But to get to this point, you need to be able to write content that cuts through the noise. Your writing won't build trust if it sounds stiff, boring, and uninspired. Your target audience won't connect with you or your business if the writing is too academic or too juvenile.

You need to learn to write content that's educational, full of personality, and relevant to your audience.

How to Attract and Engage People with Effective Content

Now that you understand why your content needs to be effective, how can you attract and engage people with your content?

Effective writing has 10 core attributes. Let's review each in more detail.

YOUR WRITING NEEDS AN ATTENTION-GRABBING HEADLINE

According to Copyblogger, 80% of people will read your headline but only 20% will read the entire article.[2] Learning how to create compelling headlines is one of the most important things you can do to improve the performance of your content efforts.

Headlines should be specific, make a promise to the reader, and if possible, prompt the viewer to read the piece right now.

Begin writing by coming up with a working title, something that will guide the structure and focus the subject of the content. This could be something like *"How to Get Past Your First Bad Idea."*

Once you finish the piece, come back to this title and refine it to be more aligned with the direction you ended up taking in the post. You might even come up with a long list of titles you can run by a colleague to get their thoughts and feedback. *It's always a good idea to get another opinion.*

For almost every piece of content, come up with at least 5 to 10 different headlines. Make it a rule that you spend at minimum five minutes brainstorming titles. It will pay off in traffic and engagement.

You can also rely on formats for headlines and titles. Let's take a look at the most commonly used formats.

There's the how-to format, which teaches the viewer how to do something. An example title could be *How to Use Excel: 14 Simple Excel Tips, Tricks, and Shortcuts.*

The list format usually follows the structure of "X ways to . . ." or examples or tips. An example title could be *30 Call-to-Action Examples You Can't Help but Click.*

The question format piques the interest of a reader and promises to answer a compelling question. An example title could be *Will "Memories" Change Snapchat as We Know It?*

The negative-angle format accuses the reader of doing something incorrectly or failing to do something—but remember that the copy should always provide a solution or the answer to your question. An example title could be *Why You Should Never Email a Proposal.*

The secret-of format provokes the curiosity of readers. An example title could be *Five Steal-Worthy Secrets of the World's Best Negotiators.*

The little-known advice, tips, or tricks format tells the reader that this advice is unique and different from what's already been published online. An example title could be

Sixteen Little-Known Google Calendar Features That'll Make You More Productive.

The you-should-know-this format reminds the reader that there is still information they don't know. An example title could be *Submitting a Guest Post? Here Are 12 Things You Should Know about Editors.*

The "interesting data" format uses a statistic to prove the value of the article. An example title could be *Only 3% of People Think Salespeople Possess This Crucial Character Trait.*

The "quick tip" format signals that it's something the reader can learn with a small time commitment. *How to Unsend an Email in Gmail [Quick Tip].*

NEXT, THE TONE NEEDS TO BE RELEVANT TO YOUR READERS

When writing for your audience, you want to match the attitude of your readers and the subject matter. Consider if your writing should be serious, fun and personable, uplifting, quirky and humorous, or authoritative. Readers might not be able to point out that the tone is what's off-putting about your content and therefore your brand, but it's the little things that can leave a big impression.

Here's an example of why tone matters so much: Simple, a company reinventing online banking, has a blog on finance and money.

The writing is anything but what you'd expect from a bank. They publish real stories from people who use money to live their lives the way they want. The writing is human, inspiring, and warm, which perfectly aligns with its goal of taking the frustration and difficulty out of dealing with a bank.

NEXT, THE CONTENT SHOULD HELP THE READER DO SOMETHING OR BETTER UNDERSTAND A TOPIC

Your blog posts, ebooks, whitepapers, and other content formats should be made with the purpose of teaching your audience how to do something or do something better. It should be useful. This is what increases your authority with your readers. To write from a helpful perspective, you need to first understand who your ideal reader is. By creating a detailed buyer persona, you'll better understand the key challenges your ideal reader faces, their pain points, how they learn new information and skills, and their goals. You can then use this information about your ideal reader to spur new content ideas or show that you understand the reader's needs in your writing.

NEXT, IT SHOULD ADD TO THE CONVERSATION, RATHER THAN REHASH WHAT'S ALREADY OUT THERE

With so much content being produced, shared, and sent each day, your content shouldn't simply restate what's already been published. It needs to add something new to the conversation, be of higher quality or more comprehensive than what already exists, answer any and all questions about the subject the reader might have, and include the most recent and relevant data for support. *Before you start writing, take a few minutes to research what already exists on the subject.* Analyze the content that is already out there. Take into consideration the depth of material, the expertise of the reader, and the perspective and stance of other writers. Ask yourself, "What's missing? What questions do I still have? How can I expand on this topic and provide more context, detail, or even entertainment?" Spend more time creating in-depth quality content rather than producing work that's easily ignored.

NEXT, WRITE THE WAY PEOPLE SEARCH

You should research the words people actually use to search and communicate. If your target reader searches for financial planning rather than wealth management, you'll naturally want to use *financial planning* in your headline and content. Use keyword research to guide you, but always default to what sounds natural and interesting to your audience.

Next, Build a Solid Structure

Effective writing makes it easy for people to follow your narrative. This all starts with having a solid structure readers recognize and, therefore, they know what to expect. For many people who skim your posts, also make sure to include interesting subheadings to draw them into a deeper reading experience.

One easy structure to use is the list formula (see Figure 5.1). Start with an intro, list the main points of the article, and then wrap it all up with a strong conclusion.

The how-to formula (Figure 5.2) is another easy-to-use and logical format. It begins with an introduction, followed by a section on why this matters to the reader that provides more context, and then details how to do something in a step-by-step format.

If you start with a formula for the backbone of your article, it's easy to get started. It can be overwhelming to write an introduction without knowing where the piece is going to go. Start by filling in the main points and *save writing the introduction and conclusion for after you've written the piece or created a solid architecture for the post.*

"List" formula

Intro
Main Subheading
1.
2.
3.
4.
5.
Subheading
Conclusion

Figure 5.1

"How-To"
formula

Intro
Why It Matters Subheading
1.
2.
3.
4.
5.
Conclusion Subheading
Conclusion

FIGURE 5.2

There's no right or wrong way when it comes to a story's structure. If you want to get creative, come up with your own formula ideas and start testing them. Just remember to keep your buyer persona's experience in mind.

NEXT, SETTLE ON ONE CORE IDEA

A clear piece of writing should have one main idea, and everything else should tie back to it. But it can be easy to lose sight of this objective once you start typing away on your keyboard. Try identifying the main objective and how the reader will benefit, and add it to the top of your draft. This should serve as a reminder to focus your content on one main idea, and it will ensure you're keeping the reader's benefit in mind as you construct your blog post or ebook. This also helps if you have an editor or a colleague editing your work before it goes live. They'll know exactly what point you're trying to get across.

NEXT, SUPPORT YOUR BRAND MESSAGING, VALUES, AND STRATEGY

Every piece of content you create and distribute should support your brand messaging—its vision, its values, and the promise you're making to your audience.

The words you use, the tone of the writing, subject matter, and details included in the content should all reinforce the reader's view of who your brand is and why the reader should want to know you better.

To make sure you're creating content with your buyer personas in mind, ask yourself how and if this content supports the buyer's journey. If it doesn't, you should question why you're writing the content in the first place.

NEXT, GIVE IT A RELEVANT CALL TO ACTION

Once you have the attention of your reader and impressed them with your inspiring and educational content, you need to tell them what you want them to do next. This can be as simple as asking the reader to share the content or write a comment in response to the post. Or it could be more direct, such as asking the audience to call a number, subscribe to your newsletter, or download a related piece of content to take with them. This is your opportunity to encourage people to continue to interact with your company, so ask for it directly, and be sure to make the conversion process as seamless and simple as possible.

Put yourself through the conversion process and ask yourself, "Is this intuitive and easy to understand?" The last thing you want is to have your audience jump through too many hoops and bounce off your site because they became overwhelmed or confused.

FINALLY, MAKE SURE IT IS FREE OF ERRORS AND POOR GRAMMAR

Effective writing is the result of a process, which usually looks like this:

1. You have an initial idea and a working title.
2. You research and collect information, data points, and quotes.
3. You perform a braindump, writing out your ideas and how-to.

4. You then start to formulate all that information into a piece of content, begin to structure the article, and remove extra or uninteresting information, which further strengthens your main objective.

5. It goes through an editing process.

This final stage is often rushed. However, this *time for refinement and polishing can be the difference between making and breaking trust.* Sloppy and wordy articles will only leave readers frustrated and feeling like they wasted their time—no matter how good the core ideas and advice are. Errors distract from your ideas and what you want to communicate to the reader.

How to Improve Your Writing

Just getting the words down on paper is a great first step. But writing 800 words versus publishing 800 words that will resonate with your readers requires a bit more work. First drafts are messy, and that's normal. When you start writing, you don't know what the final piece will look like, and you may not have a good-enough grasp of the information you need to include.

Editing requires you to cut out the unnecessary and irrelevant—anything that doesn't support your core idea. It also gives you an opportunity to refine the language to be stronger, more action-oriented. Finally, during the editing process, you ensure that the piece lacks any errors that could damage your credibility and the trust that you've built with the reader. Editing shows your audience that you care about their reading experience.

Before you move from the writing to the editing process, remember to take a break from the words. Work on something else or save the final check for when you can look at the piece with fresh ideas and a new perspective. An even better alternative is to send it to a team member who can review the content before it goes live.

Here are 10 common grammar and style points you should pay attention to before publishing your next piece of content.

FIRST, USE CONTRACTIONS

Why use contractions? They can make your writing sound less stiff and wordy.

Contractions help you sound more conversational—basically, more human—in your writing, so be sure to change words like "do not" to "don't" and "would not" to "wouldn't."

In this example, we're talking about landing-page best practices: ***Don't*** *confuse viewers with too many options on your landing pages.* ***It's*** *better to have one call to action* ***that's*** *compelling. Otherwise,* ***you'll*** *risk your prospects being confused about what they should and* ***shouldn't*** *click.*

If we were to spell out the contractions, the sentence, although not incorrect, would sound robotic and harsh, when we simply want to provide helpful advice. Here's how that same sentence would sound without contractions: ***Do not*** *confuse viewers with too many options on your landing pages.* ***It is*** *better to have one call to action* ***that is*** *compelling. Otherwise,* ***you will*** *risk your prospects being confused about what they should and* ***should not*** *click.*

NEXT, WRITE WITH SIMPLE LANGUAGE

Making your writing easier to process and understand actually makes you seem intelligent and capable. No one likes to slug through overly complex writing full of unfamiliar words. Simple language doesn't have to be boring; in fact, it can be just the opposite.

Consider this sentence: *The proliferation of social and digital channels has created a catalyst whereby a shift in the production methods by marketers is required to connect with the audience.*

That's a tough one to unpack. Although a marketer might understand this sentence, it takes extra effort to get the point, and for most, that's when readers stop paying attention.

We can relay the same message by simply stating: *The increase in the number of social and digital channels now requires marketers to create content that's not only platform-specific but also appeals to the unique audience and their behaviors on that platform.*

NEXT, USE THE ACTIVE VOICE

When you use active voice, the subject of the sentence performs an action. In passive voice, the action happens to the subject of the sentence, which can make your writing seem flat and boring.

Here's an example of passive voice: *The campaign was launched by the marketer.*

A little flat and boring, huh?

Here's the same sentence written with active voice: *The marketer launched the new campaign.*

NEXT, BE CLEAR AND CONCISE

This is the ultimate goal of editing. You have to refine the words until the point of each section, each paragraph, and each sentence is focused and clear. Clear writing requires you to have empathy for the reader—the work you produce should leave little chance for confusion or misinterpretation. One way of doing this is to remove extra words, irrelevant ideas and rants, and obvious details.

You should also use words that are familiar to your readers or provide definitions for those that are less well known. This can also mean including an analogy, metaphor, or example to clarify a complicated topic.

Let's say you have an on-call virtual nurse service and want to explain the benefits available when someone is worried about getting sick. Instead of stating this directly, you could say, "Our nurses step in with health and wellness advice when your mom isn't answering her phone." It immediately gets the point across in a way that's relatable.

> *"Creativity can solve almost any problem. The creative act, the defeat of habit by originality, overcomes everything."*
>
> This quote from George Lois, the legendary ad man who created iconic work for Xero and MTV and some of the most iconic Esquire covers, sums up why brands hire agencies. They want to tap into a group of individuals who can solve business problems with creative ideas.
>
> And agencies need to be able to depend on their staff to generate these ideas – day after day, month after month. Without this, there's not much future for their firm.
>
> But while many firms would like to think they are fostering innovation and ideas, instead they have structures, practices, and leaders who create an environment that is actually hostile to creative output.
>
> Without even realizing it, they are smothering the creative flame that attracts their clients.

FIGURE 5.3

Another way to create clarity in your writing is by putting things in context. It's one thing to share a stat on the growing adoption of a social platform, such as Snapchat, but how does this platform's growth compare with, say, Facebook or Instagram? This type of information helps to enrich the meaning of the original fact or idea.

NEXT, USE SHORT SENTENCES AND PARAGRAPHS

Break up long, dense sentences and paragraphs to make your content easier to read and comprehend.

Take, for example, the introduction from a HubSpot blog post shown in Figure 5.3.

These five paragraphs could be condensed into two paragraphs, but the breaks create white space around your writing, giving readers' eyes a rest. Most importantly, these breaks, along with varying the sentence structure and length, create rhythm, making your writing more pleasing to read.

NEXT, CUT FLUFFY WORDS

Words like "very," "really," "actually," "just," "incredibly," and "in order to" don't add anything to your sentences and can make your phrases sound bloated. You should also be careful of relying on adverbs—words ending in -ly—to describe an action, or including too many adjectives in your work. These mistakes all make for overly long, complex, and weak sentences. Run your writing through a tool like Grammarly or the Hemingway Editor to see if you can cut words or further simplify your language.

Check out this sentence: *Marketers are **very** anxious to change in order to **actually** connect with their customers before the next holiday season.*

You can cut this down to: *Marketers are anxious to change to connect with their customers before the holiday season.*

Next, Adhere to a Style Guide

Whether it's AP Style, the *Chicago Manual of Style,* or an internal style guide, use a standard set of rules to create consistency in all your communications—from your product copy to emails to ebooks to advertising. Your style guide should instruct anyone who writes on behalf of your company how to handle punctuation, grammar, voice and tone, industry-specific terms, common mistakes, and any brand-specific guidelines.

Next, Use "You" and "Your" in Your Writing

These words help you sound more conversational, like you've written the content specifically for the reader and you want to bring them into a discussion. It's important to note this is a situational recommendation. Apply the points that follow to your content if they make sense.

Many people approach writing like they're creating something for an "audience"—a vague term that brings a blurry group of people to mind—when really you should write like your favorite customer or ideal reader is sitting at their desk or on their couch reading your information. Imagine you're having a conversation or writing a letter to a respected friend. It's a simple tweak that will prevent you from sounding like you're writing an instruction manual.

Here's an example of what this sounds like: **People wanting to improve *their* overall health should start the day with a well-balanced breakfast that could include whole-grain cereal, yogurt, and egg whites. They should make time in their day to get at least 30 minutes of cardio a day, and *people* should do some type of strength training three times per week.**

A simple switch to using the second person pronoun, "you," shifts your writing to address the reader directly, making your writing sound more personable.

Let's see how that sounds with a simple perspective adjustment: *If **you** want to improve **your** overall health, try starting the day with a well-balanced breakfast that could include whole-grain cereal, yogurt, and egg whites. **You** should also make time for at least 30 minutes of cardio a day and try to do some type of strength training three times per week.*

NEXT, AVOID JARGON AND USE ACRONYMS SPARINGLY

Jargon plagues the business and marketing world. Words such as "ideation," "paradigm," "uplevel," "holistic," "disruptive," "game" "changing," "revolutionary". . . I could go on. Remember that not everyone understands the meaning behind the jargon or acronyms you rely on. Spell out acronyms at least once and try to avoid littering your content with three- and four-letter abbreviations. Imagine reading this sentence: *The **CMO** spoke to the **CTO** about the long-term **SEO** strategy to improve **PPC** metrics, such as the **CPC** and **CPL ASAP**.*

Did you get that? Probably not.

NEXT, DON'T BE SNARKY

Critical and sarcastic writing has its place, but for most businesses, this type of tone comes off negatively. Be confident and showcase your expertise, but above all, be friendly and straightforward. Sarcasm can make you look petty.

Last, Use Spell-Check

Add this to your prepublishing checklist. *It's always a good idea to double-check for spelling mistakes.* Even small errors can have a negative impact on readers' perception of your brand.

Chapter 5 Homework

Activity 1

Create a working blog post title for your next Awareness-stage content offer.

Activity 2

Open a Google Doc and create an outline for your blog post using the list formula (see Figure 5.4). Identify four to five main points that support your working title.

Activity 3

Write the first draft of your blog post.

1. Open the Google Doc you created for your blog post.
2. Expand on each main point, educating readers about why this is important.

"List" formula	Intro
	Main Subheading
	1.
	2.
	3.
	4.
	5.
	Subheading
	Conclusion

Figure 5.4

3. Remember to check for grammar and style mistakes to ensure the quality of your content.
4. Write an introduction and conclusion once the main points have been written.

ACTIVITY 4

At the top of your Google Doc, write 5 to 10 different titles for your blog post.

ACTIVITY 5

Based on your content review process, have someone review your blog post's content. Have them provide feedback on the content and choose their favorite title.

Chapter **6**

Creating a Blog Post

Why Does Blogging Help Your Business Grow?

Blogging is an effective way to regularly publish and promote new content related to your business and industry. What you'll be learning here is business blogging, which helps your content marketing in two ways:

1. It helps you attract new visitors.
2. It helps you convert those visitors into leads.

How Does It Attract New Visitors?

Think about a person searching for information online. They have questions or problems they're looking to solve. If your blog posts provide those answers, those people will find your posts, click through, and read them, turning these people into website visitors.

Every time you publish a blog post, you're creating a new, unique page online. This means you're increasing your chances of ranking high in search results, having other websites link to you, and being shared on social media. And all of this results in new traffic to your site.

Thank you to Dee Dee de Kenessey for your contribution to this chapter.

Was there a particular message that resonated well with your audience, or one that missed the mark completely? Next, you'll need to identify next steps that you can take based off the new insights you've gathered from your campaigns.

Is there a channel that you should lean into further or a tone that works best with your audience? If so, you'll want to incorporate these takeaways in future campaigns, or you can try further experimenting with these components to try boosting results.

Let's do a quick recap of all the best practices you just learned. Remember to create a content promotion calendar to help you organize your promotion plan. Then, use segmentation to create a specific audience for your content. Next, customize your message for each channel. Always be sure to experiment with new ways and promote your content and optimize for the best results. Lastly, analyze your campaign results.

If you found this information helpful and want to learn more on how to develop a well-rounded content marketing foundation, then sign up for HubSpot's free Content Marketing Certification course.

Figure 6.1

Now, How Can Your Blog Help to Convert Those New Visitors Into Leads?

Once people visit your site, you've opened the door to them. Think about it: If they're interested in your content, they're more likely to be interested in your offers and convert into leads.

Your blog can strategically promote offers from your business—anything from your latest ebook to a free consultation. *If your visitor wants to learn more, you can provide them with that next step* (see Figure 6.1).

Finally, your blog can help you stand out as an expert in your industry. The more you blog, the more people will start to look to you as a reliable, trustworthy source of information. And building that trust with your prospects will help them turn into customers down the line.

How Do You Create a Successful Blog Post?

Now that you know how blogging can help your inbound marketing, how do you create a blog post that successfully gets those results?

Let's dive into some blogging strategy and best practices.

First, Write about Your Industry, Not Yourself

Write educational content at a high level.

Remember, you're trying to attract strangers to your blog who have never heard of your company before, so they're not going to find you through search engines if you're just blogging about yourself.

Next, Brainstorm a List of Specific Topics You Could Blog About

When picking your topics, do keyword research. Which keywords do your buyer personas use? Which words are associated with your industry? Write about those topics to get found and start ranking higher in search results.

Next, Pick One Topic to Focus on per Post

Don't try to solve every problem in one fell swoop. This will make each post clearer for your readers and for search engines. It will also make sure your post gets more qualified traffic because you'll know that the people clicking through are looking for information about that specific topic.

Finally—and This Will Help Create a Long-Term Blogging Strategy—Make a List of Topics That Support a Specific Conversion

For example, if you have an ebook that you want to promote, consider making a list of blog topics that support this ebook's content. This way, if someone finds your blog post and considers the content to be helpful, the chances of them wanting to click a call to action to access a relevant offer increases. *Think of your offer as a heart and your blog posts as the arteries.* Your blog posts keep a steady flow of relevant prospects connecting with your offer.

Now, Let's Talk about Picking a Title

Think about how you read things online. You probably scan the content first, before you commit, to see if it catches your interest.

The title is one of the first things you see.

Start by creating a working title for your blog post.

Next, Include a Long-Tail Keyword in the Title

A long-tail keyword is a primary keyword—usually two to three words, like "Internet Radio Show"—that's expanded upon with additional context, such as "How to Produce an Internet Radio Show" (see Figure 6.2). Be sure the keyword fits as a description of what the page is all about.

Also, *make the value of the post clear in the title.* Your title should help readers and search engines understand what your post is about. Set the right expectations: What is the reader going to get out of your blog post? What information is covered? What format is the blog post going to take?

In Figure 6.3, the blog post's title explicitly tells you that you'll be reading about "3 tools to help you prepare for Google's next algorithm update." You know exactly what you're going to get from this blog post—how it's valuable to you, and how much information it contains.

Last, shorten the title. This is vital for search engine optimization, because Google only shows the first 50 to 60 characters of a title in search results. Avoid having your descriptive title get

Figure 6.2

FIGURE 6.3

> **11 Ways to Make Your Content Appealing to International ...**
> blog.hubspot.com/marketing/**international-content-creation** ▾   HubSpot, Inc. ▾
> Apr 14, 2015 - Learn tips for creating **content** that **appeals** to **your** entire **audience**, no matter where in the world they come from.

FIGURE 6.4

cut off. A cut-off title could ultimately hurt your click-through rate on a search engine results page.

In Figure 6.4, the title "11 Ways to Make Your Content Appealing to International Audiences" is 65 characters. You can figure out the character count by typing the title into a word processing program or by using MOZ's free title tag preview tool.[1] As you can see, this title is a little too long—the last word of the title gets cut off in the search results page.

IN THE BODY OF YOUR BLOG POST, FORMAT AND OPTIMIZE THE POST SO BOTH PEOPLE AND SEARCH ENGINES CAN EASILY READ AND UNDERSTAND IT

When you blog, white space is your friend.

White space is the empty space on the page. It allows the visitor to focus on the content, not the clutter. Don't write long paragraphs that form into huge blocks of text. This will make your information look dense and hard to read.

As you can see in Figure 6.5, there's plenty of white space on the side margins of the post, around the title and first image,

FIGURE 6.5

and between the paragraphs of text within the post. The space makes the post easily digestible—nothing is crammed together, and though the post is long, it doesn't feel overwhelming or hard to read.

You can also break up the text in your blog post by using section headers and bullets or numbered lists to highlight your points.

In this same blog post (see Figure 6.6), we have a section head, "The Advantages of Geo-Targeting," which lets the readers know what they're about to read. We have a numbered

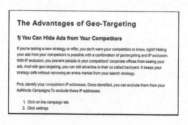

FIGURE 6.6

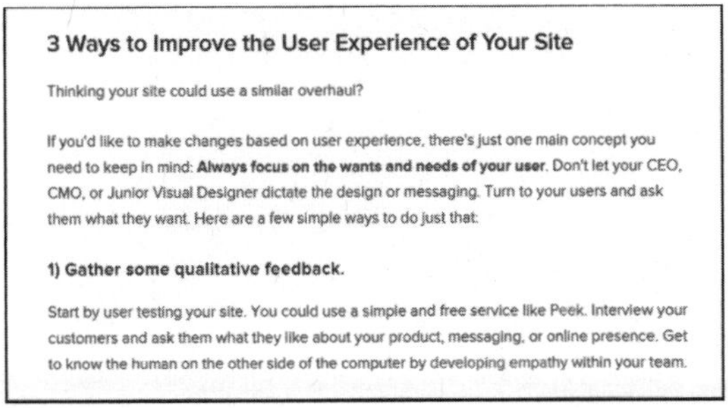

3 Ways to Improve the User Experience of Your Site

Thinking your site could use a similar overhaul?

If you'd like to make changes based on user experience, there's just one main concept you need to keep in mind: **Always focus on the wants and needs of your user.** Don't let your CEO, CMO, or Junior Visual Designer dictate the design or messaging. Turn to your users and ask them what they want. Here are a few simple ways to do just that:

1) Gather some qualitative feedback.

Start by user testing your site. You could use a simple and free service like Peek. Interview your customers and ask them what they like about your product, messaging, or online presence. Get to know the human on the other side of the computer by developing empathy within your team.

FIGURE 6.7

list as a subhead right below that, which adds some clarity; you know how the post will be structured, and it's easy to understand. And we even have another numbered list within the first section, which makes the information in the paragraphs easier to digest.

Using **bold** *type for important text can also help readers quickly understand the key takeaways from the post.*

Elements in this post (Figure 6.7) have a bold font, making it stand out, but, even more importantly, your eye catches the line "Always focus on the wants and needs of your user." This is the key takeaway from this section, so even if you skimmed, you'd still get that valuable snippet of information.

Include images to visually break up your text. Images grab attention and help your readers understand the post at a glance. Place an image at the top of every blog post to entice your visitors to read further. Your photos don't need to directly illustrate what your post is about, but they should be loosely related to your content.

And although most people enjoy a great cat photo, it may not always be relevant to your content.

NEXT, OPTIMIZE THE BLOG POST FOR SEARCH ENGINES

When search engines crawl your blog, they don't read every word. Instead, they scan certain parts of your post to

FIGURE 6.8

understand what you're writing about and how trustworthy the content is.

To help search engines understand what you're trying to communicate, *optimize the page around your long-tail keyword,* placing it in the page title and the blog post title, which are typically the same thing, and in the URL, the image alt-text, the body, and the heads.

In Figure 6.8, the long-tail keyword is "calculate value sales incentive." You can see it in the page title and post title, and in the URL for the post. Even if you can't see it here, that long-tail keyword is in the alt-text behind the image. Alt-text allows a search engine to understand what the image is about and show it in image search results.

Moving down to the body, the first paragraph reads, "There is a definite connection between sales incentives and a profitable return on investment (ROI)." You have the keywords "sales incentives" right off the bat.

Moving down, the paragraph reads, "Many times, there are intangible benefits that are difficult to measure, but just as valuable." There's the keyword "value." The next sentence, "First and foremost, there is an equation you can use to calculate your ROI," has the keyword "calculate" in it. And in the head, is "Sort out your incentives." As you can see, the post doesn't repeat the long-tail keyword over and over, so don't be afraid of breaking up your long-tail keyword or using synonyms or variations of the words. Search engines are pretty smart and will still understand what your post is about. Also include relevant internal and external links within the post. Link to related blog posts or site pages when appropriate. Although it may sound counterproductive, linking to external resources is a good idea. Google Webmasters encourage this; linking to external resources shows that you've done your research and can help bring credibility to your content. Don't go overboard, though. Link to one or two sources per paragraph at the very most.

NEXT, GENERATE LEADS—PROMOTE YOUR OFFERS ON YOUR BLOG

As you attract more and more visitors to your blog, that increased traffic means an increased opportunity to generate leads. *If you really want your content marketing efforts to pay off, it's crucial that you strategically promote the majority of your blogs to corresponding or relevant offers.*

The goal should be to attract someone and provide content around the topic they're trying to learn more about. Then be helpful and offer them a relevant next step.

Make sure the call to action (CTA) doesn't disrupt the user experience. Again, the goal is to be helpful, not pushy.

You could insert a CTA after the first few paragraphs, like the one in Figure 6.9.

To avoid looking too pushy too soon, *try including a passive CTA in hyperlinked text.* It's important to include these passive CTAs, as you can't always count on your visitor reading your entire post and converting. Think about it: When was the last time you watched a YouTube video to the end? By not including a CTA near the beginning, you may be missing out on a valuable conversion opportunity.

FIGURE 6.9

HubSpot performs CTA tests all the time. From image and text CTAs to placement of the CTAs, we're always looking for ways to improve click-through rates. Interestingly enough, we found that text CTAs near the top of blog posts produce the highest click-through rates. You might want to keep this in mind and test it on your blog posts.

LASTLY, INCLUDE A CTA AT THE END OF EACH POST

This offer should be relevant to the blog content that a visitor has just read. Your visitor is there to learn something from your blog post, so provide an offer that gives them more educational content to continue learning.

Figure 6.10 shows a CTA at the end of the same post that was shown earlier. The title of the post is "Education Blogging 101: How to Attract More Students Online," and the CTA is for a free SEO ebook targeted toward schools. The offer is about the same topic as the post, so a reader who wants to learn more would be interested in clicking through.

FIGURE 6.10

NOW THAT YOU HAVE SOME GREAT BLOG POSTS, MAKE SURE YOU'RE ALLOWING VISITORS TO EASILY SHARE THEM ON SOCIAL MEDIA

If a visitor finds one of your posts helpful and valuable, they're likely to share it to one or more of their social media channels (see Figure 6.11). More than 40 people shared this post to their LinkedIn network. If this post didn't offer social sharing buttons, it would've been a missed opportunity.

What Does a Successful Blog Post Look Like?

Let's take a look at Trade Area Systems to see what a successful blog post looks like.

This company helps retailers and shopping centers make their processes more effective and efficient (Figure 6.12).

Let's see how many best practices they've followed with their blog post, "4 Steps to Enhancing the Art of Retail Site Selection."

First, did they pick a good topic?

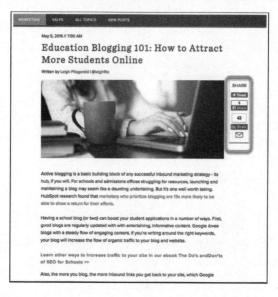

Figure 6.11

They have an educational subject: enhancing the art of retail site selection. This seems like it answers the question "How do I improve my retail site?"

Figure 6.12

Value of the post is clear

The title pops!

Trade Area Systems Blog

4 Steps to Enhancing the Art of Retail Site Selection

Share this

Long-tail keyword under 60 characters

FIGURE 6.13

And they're writing about their industry, not their company. Looking at the first few sentences, they're not mentioning Trade Area's solutions. Instead they're focusing on helping their reader learn more.

Finally, we can assume this is a topic their buyer personas want to hear about. The second line speaks right to that persona, stating, "People pick the best sites."

Next, did they choose a compelling title?

There's a long-tail keyword in the title (see Figure 6.13). A person might search for "retail site selection."

The value and structure of the blog post is clear. We're getting four steps that detail how to enhance our retail site selection.

The title pops, too. The use of the word "enhancing" brings a growth-driven, exciting element to the post.

And it's short enough—the character count is 53 characters.

Next, which formatting best practices do you see?

The post has good white space (see Figure 6.14). There's enough room to digest all of the content easily.

They also use section headers to make it easy to scan.

And they have a nice image of some paintbrushes, which is relevant to the title.

Next, is the post optimized for search engines?

They've got the long-tail keyword which is various expansions of "retail site selection," in the page title, URL, body, and

Image ——→
Whitespace
Section header ——→

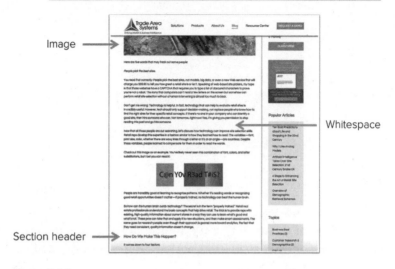

FIGURE 6.14

though you can't see it, it's behind the image in the alt-text (see Figure 6.15).

Next, are they promoting their offers?

They have a call to action (CTA) that's relevant to the topic at the bottom of the post: The "Understanding the 'Art' of Site Selection and How it Fails" white paper (see Figure 6.16).

Page title ——→
URL
Image alt-text ——→
Body

FIGURE 6.15

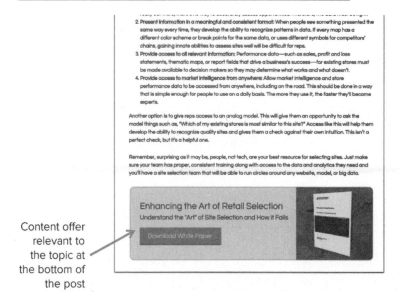

Content offer relevant to the topic at the bottom of the post

FIGURE **6.16**

Finally, are they encouraging visitors to share their post?

They have social sharing buttons at the top of the post, meaning that the reader can share this post with their personal networks.

At the end of the day, it's important to write consistently and frequently. Commit to a blogging schedule. A good place to start is creating one new blog post per week. The more often you blog, the more likely you are to get found. After all, each new blog post is an opportunity to attract new visitors and continue adding to your content savings account.

Chapter 6 Homework

Activity 1

Effective content alone isn't enough to attract search engines; you need to make sure it's optimized correctly.

Page title

URL

Image alt-text

Body

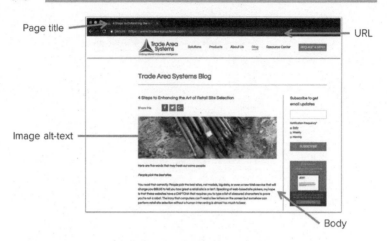

FIGURE 6.17

Figure 6.17 is an example of Trade Area System's search engine optimized blog post.

Outline the on-page SEO elements for a blog post you're working on.

1. What's the primary keyword for your blog post (generally two to three words in length)?
2. What's the long-tail keyword for your blog post (generally five words in length)?
3. What's the final title of your blog post?
4. What's the URL for your blog post?
5. What are four different synonyms of your primary keyword used within the body of your blog post?
6. What's a relevant call to action you can include to provide a helpful next step?

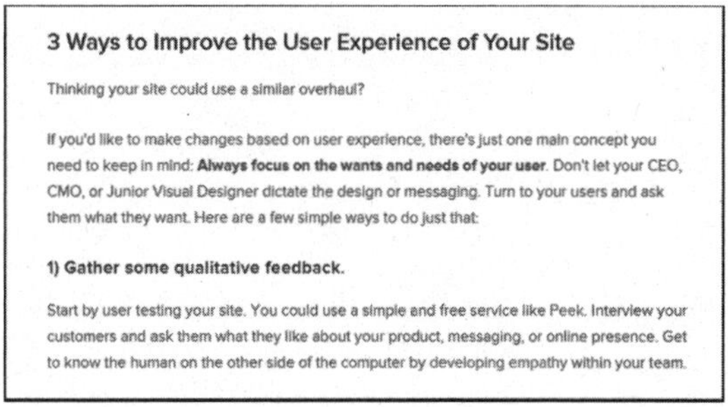

3 Ways to Improve the User Experience of Your Site

Thinking your site could use a similar overhaul?

If you'd like to make changes based on user experience, there's just one main concept you need to keep in mind: **Always focus on the wants and needs of your user**. Don't let your CEO, CMO, or Junior Visual Designer dictate the design or messaging. Turn to your users and ask them what they want. Here are a few simple ways to do just that:

1) Gather some qualitative feedback.

Start by user testing your site. You could use a simple and free service like Peek. Interview your customers and ask them what they like about your product, messaging, or online presence. Get to know the human on the other side of the computer by developing empathy within your team.

Figure 6.18

Activity 2

Using bold type for important text can also help readers quickly understand the key takeaways from the post (see Figure 6.18).

Review your blog post draft, and bold at least one key takeaway you want the reader to remember.

Chapter 7

Extending the Value of Your Content through Repurposing

Why Repurposing Content Is Important

Great content is the foundation of your content marketing plan. It attracts new visitors to your site, strengthens your online reputation, and builds trust, which ultimately leads to converting prospects into leads and eventually customers. However, it can take a lot of time and effort to create effective content on a consistent basis.

Repurposing content helps you extend the value of your content by changing it to serve a different purpose, like transforming the messaging of a blog post into a video. The messaging is the same, but the channel or format in which it's consumed is different.

There are four main benefits and advantages of repurposing content.

1. It gives you another opportunity to rank in search engines results.
2. It allows you to reach a new audience.
3. It supports the consistency of your message.

Thank you to David Arnoux for your contribution to this chapter.

4. It helps your content marketing team create content on a consistent basis.

First, It Gives You Another Opportunity to Improve Your Rank in Search Engine Results, Which Improves Your Search Engine Optimization Footprint

Content is a theme that can be showcased in different formats on various distribution channels such as YouTube, SlideShare, and your blog. Repurposing your content into new formats that fit these channels will help you secure more search engine rankings.

Second, It Allows You to Reach a New Audience

Not everyone consumes content in the same manner. Reformatting your message for a different distribution channel can get you in front of someone new who cares about what you have to say.

Third, It Supports the Consistency of Your Message

Ideas and concepts that stick aren't just said once—they're repeated over and over. Usually, buyers won't trust you the first time they come in contact with your message. The Marketing Rule of Seven is a marketing concept that states that a prospect needs to see or hear your marketing message at least seven times before they take action and buy from you. Repurposing will help you reinforce your message.

Fourth, It Helps Your Content Marketing Team Create Content on a Consistent Basis

Among B2B marketers, 50% have an issue creating content on an ongoing basis.[1] Repurposing content reduces the burden of those all-too-common "what should I write about" situations.

How Do You Extend the Value of Your Content?

Now that you know why repurposing content is important to your content marketing efforts, how do you extend the value of your content by curating it into a new format?

Let's dive into some repurposing content strategies and best practices.

There are a couple of different ways to repurpose content:

1. Republish content.
2. Recycle content.

Let's start with republishing content.

REPUBLISHING CONTENT

Content republishing is the act of reposting your content, mainly blog posts, on other websites with proper credit given to the original author. This approach allows you to focus on creating a great piece of content you can promote on other websites besides your own.

Here are three things to consider when republishing content to make sure your search engine optimization ranking isn't penalized.

First, ensure the source uses a canonical tag. This tells search engines the article is republished content—a copy of the original. This will connect search engine bots crawling the page with the original article, so they can pass the "link juice" to the appropriate website or author.

Second, make sure the repurposed content has a link at the beginning or the end of the post that connects back to your website. This is important so that new readers know where to go if they want to learn more from the original source.

Third, have the source "NoIndex" their copy of the article.   This avoids duplicate content issues by telling search engines not to rank republished content. This will not impact your rankings or the value of your inbound links.

REPUBLISHING BEST PRACTICES

There are seven best practices to consider when republishing your content.

1. There are hundreds of websites you can republish your content on, but you should strive to partner with reputable sites.
2. Don't republish all your content, just the top-performing content.
3. Take the time to update the headline of each republished piece of content.
4. Wait at least two weeks before you republish your content.
5. Include internal links throughout your post.
6. Make sure your content is a great fit for the site it's being published to.
7. Include a call to action within your post.

Let's review each in depth.

First, strive to partner with reputable sites.   Perform research to identify republishing sites relevant to your business and industry. If you're looking for a place to start, consider these:

business2community.com

socialmediatoday.com

businessinsider.com

thenextweb.com

huffingtonpost.com

quora.com

reddit.com

Websites with a high domain authority will give you a stronger lift in search engine rankings.

Additionally, there are sites where you can republish your content and manage it, like LinkedIn, Medium, and Inbound .org. These sites make it easy to control the messaging and timing of your posts.

Second, don't republish all your content, just the top-performing content. Not all of your content is going to produce high results. Only republish your best-performing content; if the content performed well on your blog, chances are it will perform well on other sites.

Third, take the time to update the headline of each republished piece of content. This will help each post stand out, especially when someone performs a search query. They'll see multiple variations of your content, keeping it fresh.

When marketer and entrepreneur Ryan Battles publishes a blog post, he republishes it to LinkedIn, Medium, Reddit, and other relevant channels, thereby maximizing the reach of his content (see Figure 7.1).[2] But here's the kicker: He alters the headline of the republished articles to differ from the original blog post.

FIGURE 7.1

Notice Battle's blog post headline on his website: "Finding Your Customer's Pain Points."

Then see how the content is republished to LinkedIn and Reddit with the headline "Nailing Your Audience's Pain Points."

Fourth, wait at least two weeks before you republish your content. You want to give search engines enough time to index the original piece of content so that it ranks higher than the republished content.

Fifth, include internal links throughout your post. This will give readers the opportunity to learn more about specific products, services, or other pieces of content you have to offer.

Notice that when you click through to Battle's post on LinkedIn, there's a link in the first sentence at the phrase "knowing your audience" (see Figure 7.2). When clicked, it takes you to a relevant article on his website about knowing your audience.

Figure **7.2**

Sixth, make sure your content is a great fit for the site it's being published to. If there isn't a section that's relevant to what you're writing about, then it's not a good fit, and the value isn't there.

Finally, include a call to action within your post. Remember, blog posts are a great tool to convert visitors into leads. Not including a relevant call to action (CTA) is a missed opportunity.

Scrolling down Battle's post—see Figures 7.3 and 7.4— you'll notice he uses a hierarchy of helpful calls to action.

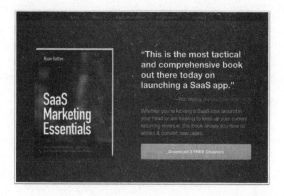

FIGURE 7.3

FIGURE 7.4

RECYCLING CONTENT

Now that we know how to republish content, let's take a look at how to recycle it.

Recycling content isn't as simple as copying and pasting material from one content format to another. If you want effective recycled content, then you'll want to use the ACE method, which stands for:

- ◆ Adjust
- ◆ Combine
- ◆ Expand

To start, you may need to adjust your content to make sure it provides a good user experience. Ask yourself questions like "What needs to be added, removed, or reworded?"

Next, consider combining related or unrelated content to provide new value or meaning.

Last, is there an opportunity to expand on something you've already done in order to dig deeper into that topic? Think about a comprehensive, big-picture view.

Keeping these three things in mind, let's see how we can put them into action.

When recycling content, think from the ground up, like the growth of a tree. Every healthy tree has roots, a trunk, and a crown that's made up of multiple branches, as shown in Figure 7.5.

Think of your roots as a series of short-form content, like blog posts, social messages, and videos.

The purpose of a tree's roots is to form connections and bond with other roots to grow into a tree, which produces a trunk. Think of the trunk as a long-form content offer, like a guide or ebook.

And what grows from the trunk? Branches! Think of each branch as an extension of your content offer into a new format, like a webinar or infographic.

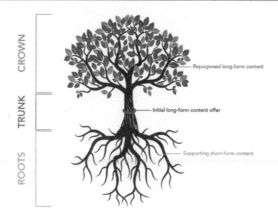

FIGURE 7.5

Your content marketing plan should be filled with a forest of trees that have strong roots and branches.

Interesting concept, right? But how do you do it?

What you need is an end goal, something that other initiatives can grow into. If you have an end goal, like publishing a comprehensive guide, then weekly content creation activities like social media and blogging can serve a much larger purpose to support your overall content marketing plan.

Don't create content just to create content.

If your goal is to attract, convert, close, and delight your potential prospects, turning them into valuable customers, look to the buyer's journey and your buyer persona. *Think of each content idea that provides value to your buyer persona as a seed.*

This seed is something that can be planted, and if you consistently nurture that seed, really giving it the attention it needs and deserves, it will sprout and start to develop a foundation of roots that will grow into a healthy sapling. And if you continue to nurture it, that sapling will go on to develop into a mature tree with strong branches.

Identifying content in the buyer's journey will help cultivate strong seeds for your content creation efforts.

To Understand This Concept, Let's Build a Comprehensive Guide by Identifying the Seed First

To create your seed, you need to have an idea that you care about—something that you're willing to nurture and help flourish. Here's how I did it.

My wife, Ariele, and I are wanderers. We've moved around from state to state and realized this is a lifestyle that suits us well. Through our journeys, we've learned how to repurpose everything in our lives to reduce clutter, including our truck, George.

George is a 2009 Ford F-250 Super Duty work truck. George may look like your average work truck with a cap over the truck bed, but looks can be deceiving—he's much more than that.

I'm someone who loves to stretch the value out of things, so Ariele and I decided to repurpose George into a storage unit that doubles as a camper.

Our goal was to help other like-minded minimalists by documenting our experience and creating an in-depth, step-by-step guide to help them convert their vehicle into a functional living space.

Here's how *we created a 76-page guide* during the span of two months using Instagram, YouTube, and our blog, wildwewander.com/journal.

First, we identified the format and topic for the content—a step-by-step guide on how to convert a truck into a diy truck camper. The topic "DIY truck camper" was the overarching idea of what we wanted to write about. This idea was the seed for the tree we wanted to produce (Figure 7.6). We had to identify this before planting and growing the roots.

Next, we made a list of subtopics that supported the overarching topic. The important thing to consider here is choosing subtopics that are strong enough to provide value by

FIGURE 7.6

themselves. For us, this was "creating an off-grid electrical system" and "weatherizing your truck cap." But these subtopics also need to complement the other subtopics in your comprehensive guide.

These subtopics are our roots (Figure 7.7). We need them to grow into a strong, compelling offer.

One thing to keep in mind when identifying supporting subtopics is to *make a list of as many ideas as possible* (see Figure 7.8). The more subtopics you can identify, the better, as this list is only going to strengthen your roots. But don't feel that you

FIGURE 7.7

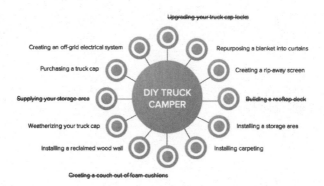

FIGURE 7.8

need to recycle each subtopic into the content offer. Just choose the strongest, most relevant subtopics to create your initial content offer from. If you have extra topics, use them down the road for potential content ideas in support of the overarching topic.

Notice how we identified "building a rooftop deck" as a supporting topic but decided not to include it in the guide. I attempted multiple variations of the rooftop deck build but just couldn't get it right. Instead of letting that subtopic bog down progress, we decided to leave it off the list and work on it later.

This is the outline for our guide. Now we can focus on creating content for each subtopic as opposed to thinking about the entire guide, which makes this process much more manageable.

Next, we started the project and documented our progress on instagram. We chose Instagram because it's our primary social media channel where we engage with our audience. You could do the same with Facebook, Twitter, or Snapchat.

Next, we wrote a blog post for each subtopic. And because we knew we were going to need visual aids for each post, we embedded Instagram photos throughout each blog post.

Next, we created a video for each blog post. We hosted the videos on YouTube and embedded them at the end of each blog post.

This was a nice value-add for readers, because it gave them the opportunity to view the progress after reading about it. Again, the video content follows the same story of our Instagram page and our blog, but it's in a different content format on a different distribution channel.

Let's take a look at a blog post about repurposing a blanket into a ceiling cover and curtains (Figure 7.9). See how we used Instagram photos and videos to help tell the story.

FIGURE 7.9

Scrolling down the blog post, notice how we inserted a YouTube video at the end of the post (Figure 7.10).

Are you noticing a trend here? Not only have we told a cohesive story across multiple channels, but also, and more important, we've integrated all the content formats. Readers now know what other channels we have and can choose to engage with and follow us there as well.

Once we had all of the content for the guide, we downloaded a free ebook template from HubSpot's marketing resources library, which is free to all.[3]

From resources about lead generation to building editorial calendars, there's something for every content marketer in the resources library.

We recycled blog posts, instagram photos, and YouTube videos to help build our comprehensive guide. And while we could have just copy-and-pasted the blog content, we

Lastly, install the tailgate curtain.

Start by connecting blanket ends where the VELCRO hook and loop meet to complete the ceiling cover.

Connect the blanket to the aluminum framing above the tailgate. Make sure the blanket is nice and tight from the adjoining ceiling-to-tailgate connection.

If you were able to find a blanket that covers the entire area of the ceiling, then you can skip the above step.

Next connect the VELCRO adjoining strips to their counterparts above the tail gate and let the blanket hang down to the floor.

And there you have it. Making use of a blanket as curtains and a ceiling cover in your truck to mobile micro camp project.

Want to see how this project turned out? Check out the video tour below:

FIGURE 7.10

adjusted and expanded the blog posts' content to provide additional context and value within the guide.

All we needed to do to complete the guide's content was add an introduction and a conclusion. Effective writers often wait to do these tasks last.

By nurturing the continuous growth of these roots, we grew them into our step-by-step guide (Figure 7.11).

Once we finalized the guide's content, the next step was to create a cover. For your guide, take the time to create a cover that pops. Have you ever heard the phrase "don't judge a book by its cover"? Well, *people are definitely judging your*

FIGURE 7.11

From Truck Cap
TO
Truck Camper

JUSTIN • ARIELE CHAMPION

Learn how we converted our truck into a DIY truck camper.

FIGURE 7.12

downloads by their covers. In fact, 79% of people said the cover was an important part of the decision-making process.[4]

Keeping this in mind, we worked with a designer to create a transformational-focused cover (Figure 7.12). This kind of cover helped viewers see the before and after of the project.

And there you have it—an effective way to form a compelling long-form offer by recycling short-form content tasks.

But we're not done yet! We still have to connect all the content we created with links. Links help search engines, as well as people, easily find the content we're trying to put in front of them.

Each blog post was created before the offer launched, so we didn't have a relevant CTA to offer. Instead of leaving out the CTA, we allowed visitors to subscribe to email updates. This way, we could promote the guide to them once it was available.

To promote the offer after it was launched, we went back to each blog post and inserted an image CTA with descriptive alt text for search engines to read.

This framework can work for any type of content offer you want to create. You just need to *take the time to plan the contents of your offer so you can make use of your weekly content tasks.*

Once you have a content offer, start thinking about how you can reuse this content. You can draw a great deal of value by branching it out into additional content formats.

Ask yourself, "How else might this content be consumed?" If you're looking for a place to start, consider looking to your buyer's journey. Not only will this help ensure you're creating content with a purpose, but also, and more importantly, this will help keep your message consistent throughout each stage of the buyer's journey.

To help you understand this, let's recap our guide example (Figure 7.13). We identified the content format and topic of an offer we wanted to create; we built a foundation through a series of Instagram posts, videos, and blog posts; and we recycled that content into a comprehensive guide.

Now let's consider how we could branch out this content into new formats for our buyer personas to consume (Figure 7.14).

To start, what about recycling the guide into a slide deck? We could take key information from each chapter and create a

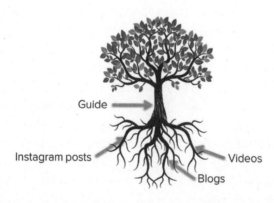

FIGURE 7.13

Figure 7.14

slide for it. This would condense the information while still communicating the value in a visual way.

And we could take our slide deck and post it to SlideShare.

Now that we have a slide deck, what about recycling it and using it to host a digital training or a webinar? This could be a great opportunity to create an engaging learning experience for our audience, one where they have the opportunity to ask questions and learn more about our thought leadership and what we have to offer. And we could offer a recording of the webinar on our website, or upload it to YouTube and Vimeo.

What about recycling the slide deck into an infographic? Infographics are a great way to visually tell a story. They're also great attention drivers that could help get the word out about the guide.

We could even write a blog post about the infographic, and share it across all our social media channels.

What about recycling our infographic into a videographic by animating it and adding a voiceover to provide additional context?

We could upload the videographic to YouTube and Vimeo, write a blog post about it, and share it across all our social media channels.

We could even take it a step further and launch a content series that's released over time.

What about recycling our guide into an email series? We could help organize the project by splitting up each chapter into a series of emails over a specific span of time. This could make the content more digestible than reading it all at once.

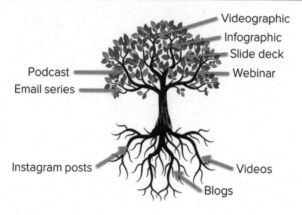

Videographic
Infographic
Slide deck
Podcast
Email series
Webinar
Instagram posts
Videos
Blogs

Figure 7.15

We could offer a landing page that allows people to subscribe to the email series.

What about recycling the email series into a podcast? We could recycle the email content into audio episodes. This way, people could listen to our content while actually doing the project.

That's right—we're still going (Figure 7.15).

We could also offer a landing page that allows people to subscribe to the podcast and host through Soundcloud, Podbean, or iTunes.

As for our example, after going through this process and making many trips to the hardware store for materials and tools, we decided to first recycle the guide into a checklist.

This way, if the reader wants to get started, they have everything they need to stay organized. I really could have used a checklist during our build.

And because we used the content from the guide to create the checklist, it only took us a few hours to complete. That's what I like to call efficiency.

The opportunities to recycling content are endless. Just make sure to always tie content creation back to the buyer persona and the buyer's journey to make sure it supports your topic.

What's an Example of Repurposing Content?

Let's take a look at a company called Growth Tribe to learn how they successfully repurposed content into a new product for their company.

Growth Tribe offers technical marketing training for graduates and professionals. They're building an international brand that stands for cutting-edge knowledge. And with their small team of 15, they have limited resources to create content. So they want to create content that works and that can be recycled over and over again.

Growth Tribe performs a lot of presentations, and for one upcoming presentation, they spent hours researching a specific topic: growth hacking. Part of that research involved collecting and reading a large number of online articles. In this case, it was 50 or 60 articles. They also bookmarked 150 of their favorite articles that were relevant to this topic. This list of articles was high quality and organized by category, but it didn't provide the best user experience.

What initially looked like only a bunch of links was actually something that had the potential to be an epic curated resource list.

But how do they promote this list? Should they simply tweet it or put it on their blog? No. They took things a little bit further—they got creative.

Growth Tribe discovered a platform called ZEEF that allows you to create blocks of links based on certain categories. And ZEEF pages have a good level of traffic. This could be a good showcase for Growth Tribe's list of curated links (see Figure 7.16).

ZEEF pages have some basic statistics attached to them, and the people at Growth Tribe saw that the number of links on their pages was quickly growing. This meant there was interest for this type of resource.

Growth Tribe calls this "initial traction." Eventually, they were featured on ZEEF's homepage, which gave their blog a healthy boost in traffic.

Figure 7.16

Growth Tribe then asked themselves if it would be possible to host this ZEEF page on their website. And it was. So they embedded the ZEEF list of curated links onto their website, and they now have an extra landing page dedicated to this resource list (Figure 7.17).

The list started to receive a significant number of views—upward of 1,000 views per week—thanks to shares and proper

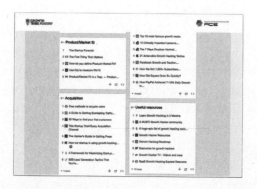

Figure 7.17

search engine optimization. This was an early signal that they had quality content in their possession. So how did they repurpose this content even more?

Growth Tribe decided to recycle this one-page resource list into an email course.

They broke up the content into a more digestible format to be consumed over multiple weeks. Sure, this would require some time to create, but they already had the early signals that this content was useful for their target audience. Now, after signing up for a free email course, visitors could receive a weekly email with the most interesting articles, as well as a top tool or a top trick at the bottom of the email. *This was essentially the exact same content as the resource list, with a little bit added to increase its value;* Growth Tribe upgraded the content and published it in a different format.

The Growth Tribe team quickly reached their first 2,000 subscribers. They decided to give the email course its own landing page, and they started to promote it as a separate product (see Figure 7.18).

What started out as a small list of links actually became a separate product that helped the business acquire thousands of valuable new subscribers.

Growth Tribe realized that all the content categories they created were, in fact, the skills necessary to become a techni-

FIGURE 7.18

FIGURE 7.19

FIGURE 7.19

cal marketer, also known as a growth marketer. The next step was to recycle these categories into a piece of engineered marketing. So they took it one step further and created a growth hacking grader (Figure 7.19) that actually grades your skills.

Chapter 7 Homework

ACTIVITY 1

Write down the format (e.g., ebook, guide) and topic for a long-form piece of content. *Consider using the Awareness-stage guide or ebook you identified in Chapter 4, "Planning a Long-Term Content Strategy."* Think of the topic as you would a working title—what do you want to communicate?

ACTIVITY 2

Identify five supporting short-form subtopics for your content offer. Each supporting subtopic should be strong enough to be a stand-alone piece, but when combined with other supporting subtopics, it should build your long-form content resource. For each, write down the subtopic and write a brief explanation of it.

Pro tip: Look to your content audit to see what content you already have that you might be able to repurpose as a subtopic in your guide (there's no use reinventing the wheel if you already have valuable content in your possession).

ACTIVITY 3
Create a blog post for each supporting subtopic you need to bring the guide to life. Complete this activity based on your and your team's bandwidth. You can write them all at once, or you can spread them out over time by making sense of your weekly content tasks.

ACTIVITY 4
Create a template for your guide. If you don't already have a template, go to this link and download one for free: https://www.hubspot.com/resources.

    Pro tip: Take the time to create a custom cover that catches the attention of your reader. If you need help getting started, consider this simple graphic design software: https://www.canva.com.

Chapter **8**

How to Effectively Promote Content

Why Content Promotion Is Important

Take a moment to reflect on the last great piece of content you came across. Maybe it was a book, an infographic, an email, or even a video.

Now, how did you discover that piece of content? Did a friend send it to you or make a recommendation? Did it pop up in your social media newsfeed or timeline?

No matter how you discovered the last piece of content you consumed, each one is an example of content promotion. What is content promotion? Well, it's the distribution of content through a variety of media channels. Some channels include social media networks, blogs, emails, and live events, just to name a few.

As a content marketer, it's important to understand how to leverage promotion channels to connect with new audience members and prospects.

And, as a content marketer, you probably spend a lot of time creating remarkable content in the hopes of helping others

---

Thank you to Markiesha Ollison and Kit Lyman for your contributions to this chapter.

find solutions to be successful. Maybe it's for a company, for a client, or even for your own personal needs. Now, imagine you were never able to share your solutions or knowledge with the people who needed it most.

How devastating would that be? It'd be as if you were a scientist who made a ground-breaking discovery, but the results never made it out of the lab.

When it comes to content, create less and promote more. Think about it—you wouldn't spend your entire time planning an event, like a birthday party, without promoting it. What would be the point if no one showed up?

With content promotion, you're able to get your message to the people who need it the most.

Once your remarkable content has converted viewers into leads, you'll be able to personally deliver content at the times and places your buyer persona needs it the most. Content promotion can also help communicate the value they'd receive as your customer, while also nurturing relationships to turn your customers into delighted, lifelong promoters.

Let's not forget to mention the true value that content promotion can have for your business.

In 2016, it was reported that 47% of B2B buyers consume three to five pieces of content prior to engaging with a salesperson.[1] This could mean that nearly half of your customers were consuming your content before your sales team even knew who they were.

But seriously, content promotion can drive website traffic, improve engagement from audience members, prospects, and customers, and aid buyers in making purchase decisions with your business.

Now that we've discussed why content promotion is essential to your content strategy, let's dive deeper into content promotion techniques that will help you excel at promoting your high-quality work.

Organic versus Paid Content Promotion

Before diving into content promotion best practices, it's important to understand the relationship between organic content promotion and paid content promotion.

Organic content promotion is designed to increase the visibility of your content and the effectiveness of your marketing campaigns without spending money on ad space, boosted content, or promoted content.

Some of the most effective organic content promotion channels are:

♦ Search engine optimization
♦ Email marketing
♦ Live promotions, like events or webinars
♦ Influencer networks
♦ Good ol' fashioned word of mouth

A benefit of doing organic promotion is increased brand authority across various platforms. Because the amount of content you can promote isn't limited by a budget, you're able to use multiple platforms to promote quality content and increase awareness about your business and brand. However, the challenge is that *you'll need to ensure consistency around developing and publishing content regularly.*

In contrast, paid content promotion allows you to show your content to a highly specific audience. In most cases, you're able to customize the target audience pool as well as the message, but you'll have to spend money in order for anyone to see your content.

The most common channels for paid promotion are search engine ads that are placed on platforms, such as Google, Yahoo!, or Bing, and paid social media campaigns on platforms, such as Facebook, LinkedIn, Twitter, and Instagram.

A benefit of paid promotion is the ability to develop and deliver highly targeted content to consumers who'll find the content most relevant. A challenge when doing paid promotion is securing enough budget to achieve your desired results. To overcome this challenge, it's best to experiment with a small budget to discover the best ways to achieve your desired outcome.

The most efficient way for organic and paid content promotion to work together is by promoting well-performing content. Content that performs well will have above-average engagement, such as likes, shares, retweets, and link clicks, which will drive traffic to your website. Platforms like Facebook make this easy to understand, because they'll tell you when you have a high-performing post and recommend that you increase its reach with ad spend.

As a result, you'll be more effective at increasing the reach of your content, attracting new audience members and prospects, and helping leads make better decisions about your business.

Be careful, though—not all top-performing posts are created equal. With social platforms often pushing advertisers toward impression-based ads, using high-converting content becomes even more crucial. If you're going to boost a social media update with ad dollars, you better make sure it's worth it.

Let's take a look at an example Facebook post from a small, family-owned business, Mountain Mystic Company (Figure 8.1).

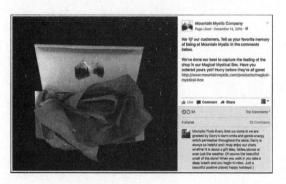

FIGURE 8.1

In this post, Mountain Mystic is announcing their Magical Mystical Box, an item they created to capture the feeling of being in their shop for those who have never been in before. As you can see, this post has:

♦ An image of the product
♦ A clear call to action
♦ A link to view their product, the Magical Mystical Box

However, *what's interesting about this post is that it's not focused on the box as much as it is on the audience's experience of being in the shop.* Notice the first paragraph: "We love our customers. Tell us your favorite memory of being at Mountain Mystic in the comments field below."

They're talking to their audience in a human way, letting them know how much they appreciate them. Yes, they explain what they're offering in the second paragraph, but they're focusing on their audience first, making it conversational.

The post started to gain traction, so Mountain Mystic promoted their product to their audience of 1,700 followers for less than $25. The result? Thirty-five valuable comments and over 200 engagements from others explaining their experiences of visiting Mountain Mystic. Most commenters even went above and beyond to explain why they love the shop. At the time, this was a record-engaging post for Mountain Mystic.

As for their ecommerce test, Mountain Mystic sold out of all their Magical Mystical Boxes during preorder.

Now that you understand the powerful relationship between organic and paid content promotion, let's discuss the best practices that will help you excel at using them together.

Here's a list of content promotion best practices we'll review.

♦ Create a content promotion calendar to help keep things organized.

- Segment your content.
- Customize your message for each channel.
- Experiment and optimize for performance.
- Analyze the results to find new opportunities.

How to Excel at Content Promotion

Developing a successful content promotion strategy may sound easy, but it does require some work. Let's be honest, if success was as easy as posting a few tweets or sending an email or two out to the masses, then more than 42% of B2B marketers would say they're effective at content marketing.[2]

So, we're going to discuss how you can excel at content promotion and the best practices that will help you deliver your content across multiple channels and achieve the results you need.

First, Use a Content Promotion Calendar

A content promotion calendar will help you keep track of various types of communications and the dates and times for when they'll be published. However, this calendar is not one-size-fits-all, which is why it's important to create a promotion plan that will include details about your target audiences, internal and external communication channels, and the content that will be distributed across these channels. The content promotion calendar ties all these details together to create a game plan for how and when communications will be released.

Think of your promotion calendar as an itinerary for your content. Imagine you're planning a trip to a new country. How would you keep track of the places you'd like to visit, the transportation you'd use to get there, or even your times of departure and arrival? An itinerary helps keep you organized, and your content promotion calendar will do the same.

SECOND, USE SEGMENTATION TO CREATE A SPECIFIC AUDIENCE TO RECEIVE YOUR CONTENT

Segmentation is a powerful best practice to use when promoting content across multiple channels. Segmentation is used to divide large audiences or target markets into smaller segments based on specific criteria. It's a helpful step that makes it easier for you to target the right people for your business and avoid showing ads or serving content to people who are ultimately not a good fit. When you use segmentation, always keep your buyer persona in mind and create segments that align with the interests, demographics, and geographical location of your ideal customer.

Your ability to segment your audience will vary depending on the promotion channel you use. Often, content marketers use segmentation for email marketing campaigns, social media campaigns, and paid campaigns.

Segmentation in email is typically done using lists with specific criteria for contacts in a company's database. The criteria in your list is based on preexisting information you've collected from your contacts; this could be through analytics or questions you've asked them on a form. Social media campaigns can target audience members based on information contained in a user's online profile, such as their interests, the city where they live, education, as well as lifestyle and interest traits, like cooking or hiking.

Paid media campaigns take segmentation even further, by allowing you to target audience members outside your social network and who may have never heard of your business. Platforms like Google Display Network allow you to put your content in front of audiences on websites that are relevant to your business. If you're a company like Airbnb, which offers worldwide accommodations, then showing your content on sites that talk about travel, adventure, and being outdoors may be good places to promote your brand.

By using segmentation, you'll be creating a custom audience for your content, but it will also make it easy to create a customized message for audience members across all of your channels.

Third, Create a Custom Message for Each Channel

When developing your message, there are a few things you'll need to keep in mind. The first is the tone of your message.

Tone is defined as the general attitude of your message. When deciding the tone, think about the feeling you want your message to carry. It should be closely aligned with the tone of your content, but they're not always the same thing. You may want your message to inspire your audience, encourage them, educate them, or maybe just make them laugh.

Another thing to consider when developing your message is how you will clearly communicate the value of the content you're promoting. You want to be sure to not oversell the value of your content or promise more than what will be delivered. You also don't want to undersell the value of your content, which can result in missed opportunities for your business.

One way to check if you're communicating the true value of your offer is to define two to three benefits someone would gain from your piece of content and try using at least one of them in the message you'll use to promote it.

You'll also want to customize your message to match the distribution channel, as each channel has a unique audience that expects content to be delivered in a specific way.

For example, if you're delivering content on a social media platform, you can explore new and creative ways of delivering your messaging.

From witty messages to fun GIFs and short videos, you can test ways to deliver the most powerful message that will resonate with your audience and get the most engagement.

Email, on the other hand, is a bit more personal, so your message should be highly customized to the individual who's receiving it. You can include information like name, company, or job title as elements that will help personalize your message.

The important thing to keep in mind is that each message you create to promote your content is like an invitation for audience members to engage with your business. As a result, you want to do your best to personalize each message for every recipient.

FOURTH, EXPERIMENT AND OPTIMIZE

Experimentation is a great way to learn how to best deliver your content to your audience, and it's something you should be doing on a consistent basis. There's no magic recipe for how to promote a piece of content. Instead, you'll need to try new ingredients by testing new content promotion tactics.

You may want to experiment with the message, the distribution channel, the time of day, the day of the week, and paid versus organic promotion. Treat each of these areas like a variable in an A/B test. *You only want to change one variable per experiment.* This means if you're running a campaign to promote your newest ebook, you may want to experiment with changing the messaging to find one that gets the most engagement. This will help you be more effective and efficient when repurposing that message on other platforms.

Optimization is a little different.

Optimization is used to achieve the best possible outcome for your promotion plan. When it comes to content promotion, there are three key areas you want to optimize: reach, engagements, and conversions.

Reach is used to measure the size of your potential audience. This includes people who are directly and indirectly in your social network. Optimizing for reach helps you get the most potential eyes on your content. Think of this as the top of your content promotion funnel. You want to grow your reach as far and wide as possible while still remaining relevant.

How can you optimize for reach? Get your content in as many places as possible, include a link in your email signature, share the content on social media, and encourage your network to share the content with their networks. Reach out to influencers in your industry or community, either through social media, email, or in person, and encourage them to share your content. *The key is to always tell people about your content.*

Engagement measures the number of interactions with your brand, such as likes and shares. When you optimize for engagement, start by considering how a user is going to engage with that piece of content. Will they be reading it? Watching it? Or simply downloading it for another time? Will they be scrolling through your content on their desktop or their phone? Do they engage by leaving a comment, sending it to a colleague, or clicking a link?

Once you have this information, you can modify your messaging to include relevant action words and visuals, perhaps even making adjustments based on the platform being used to view the content. Keep in mind that some of these changes may take time, so be patient.

Optimizing your content for conversions requires you to have a clear definition of what a conversion for your content type is and an understanding of how your promotion channels impact the conversion process. Conversions may be downloads, views, trials, demos, sign-ups, and the list goes on. To optimize for conversions in your promotion strategy, you'll need to use a link to a landing page or website page with a relevant conversion action. Doing so will help you convert that website visitor into a lead for your business.

But remember, *don't make every social media post about offers you're trying to extend to your audience.* The goal is to build a relationship and trust with those you reach. No one likes that person at a party who's constantly talking about themselves.

When promoting your content on social media, consider the 10-4-1 rule. This rule serves as a guideline for the content you publish on social media. It'll help you ensure people don't tune out over a 15-post period. Here's an overview of the 10-4-1 rule.

10: Publish 10 posts promoting content from a relevant third-party website. This will help increase your credibility as an information hub in your industry.

4: Publish 4 posts promoting original content created by your business. This could be blogs, videos, or anything else that will educate your reader.

1: Publish 1 post supporting an offer, such as a guide or white paper. If you follow the 10-4-1 rule, then you've earned the right to sell something to your audience.

AFTER YOU'VE RUN A SUCCESSFUL PROMOTION CAMPAIGN, IT WILL BE TIME FOR YOU TO ANALYZE THE RESULTS OF YOUR EFFORTS, WHICH IS THE FIFTH BEST PRACTICE

To start, you'll want to analyze the performance of your promotions' channels. Is there one or two that exceeded expectations? Or maybe there's one channel that significantly underperformed? Once you've identified these trends, you'll want to explore each channel individually and assess how each message impacted the overall performance of the channels. Was there a particular message that resonated well with your audience, or one that missed the mark completely?

Next, you'll need to identify steps you can take based on the new insights you've gathered from your campaigns.

Is there a channel you should lean into or a tone that works best with your audience? If so, you'll want to incorporate these takeaways into future campaigns, or you can try further experimenting with these components to boost results.

What a Successful Content Promotion Campaign Looks Like

Let's take a look at an inbound marketing agency, SmartBug Media, and how they successfully promoted an Awareness-stage guide to their primary buyer persona, Marketing Mary.

The company is well known for helping their clients increase leads, customers, and revenue by using content marketing and inbound marketing strategies. How do they do it? Well, they create content on a consistent basis that brings value and educates their ideal readers. What better way of selling your services than putting it into action?

Before we dive in, here's an overview of SmartBug's buyer persona, Marketing Mary.

Mary's a traditional marketer at the management level who wants to prove the importance of her job through return on investment (ROI). Through this process, she also wants to create memorable campaigns, something that she's proud of putting her name on.

Mary's biggest challenge is that she's new to content and inbound marketing but is eager to learn more. Mary generally shuts off at the end of the day to spend more time with family but is very productive and efficient while at work.

She would seek help from SmartBug to get more of her time back, create more content, and prove marketing ROI so she looks like a marketing rockstar.

Keeping Mary's attributes in mind, SmartBug created an Awareness-stage content offer titled "The Ultimate Guide to Inbound Marketing Personas" (Figure 8.2).

The guide is a comprehensive 34-page resource that provides information on why personas matter, how more details lead to bigger dividends, how to extract valuable details from marketing and sales teams (and your customers), as well as 75 development questions covering demographics, career, daily life, habits, pain points, and more.

This is definitely a resource that would interest Mary and bring value to her knowledge search on why to develop buyer personas.

And while all this information would help Mary, she's only going to find it if SmartBug spreads the word, which they did.

First, SmartBug recycled content from the guide into a relevant blog post series.

FIGURE 8.2

Figure 8.3 shows blog post SmartBug used to attract Mary: "55 Questions to Ask When Developing Buyer Personas." The content in this blog post is similar to what's offered in the guide. This helps make the call to action (CTA) at the end of the blog post that much more relevant. If someone found the blog post helpful, they're likely to download the guide.

Next, SmartBug promoted the guide week after week on their social media channels by using snippets of content from the guide to keep each post fresh. Take the tweet shown in Figure 8.4, for example. It explains persona development tip #44: "What are the top questions asked by prospects?"

Notice how SmartBug included an image, a link to the guide, and a hashtag—#75daysofpersonas—to track the campaign's results. Very smart.

SmartBug then launched targeted social ads to promote the guide to a new and relevant audience. Check out this Facebook

Figure 8.3

ad shown in Figure 8.5. Notice how it offers context about the guide, a link to access it, and an image of what it looks like.

SmartBug continued by using email to promote the guide to their email subscriber list. In Figure 8.6, notice how SmartBug

Figure 8.4

FIGURE 8.5

highlights the problem and solution in red and uses an image CTA to drive attention to the helpful next step.

That's great and all, but how did this guide perform?

Well, the landing page for the guide has been *viewed over 8,000 times with a conversion rate of almost 44%, of which 30% are all new contacts.*

FIGURE 8.6

FIGURE **8.7**

Seeing how well this content was received by their audience, SmartBug wanted to keep up the pace, so they started recycling the content from the guide into other long-form pieces of content, like a SlideShare deck (see Figure 8.7). Not only did this help from a search engine optimization perspective, by claiming more search engine real estate, but more importantly, it allowed them to reach a new audience.

And there you have it—a successful content promotion campaign in action. Although this was designed for SmartBug's persona Marketing Mary, remember that every industry and persona is different. You'll want to develop a promotion strategy of your own that meets your and your audience's needs.

Chapter 8 Homework

Activity 1

Each promotion channel provides a different user experience. Simply copying and pasting the same message across all your channels may save you time, but it won't provide the best experience for your audience. Furthermore, you'll be missing an opportunity to optimize messaging based on the specific marketing channel.

Select a recent blog post your business published and write a unique promotion message for at least three of your marketing channels like Facebook, Twitter, or email.

Remember, each channel offers a different user experience. The goal is to tailor the message to the user experience on that channel.

Activity 2

You spend a lot of time creating content to only share it on social media once. So, you can easily share the same piece of content multiple times without deterring folks by refreshing the social post's messaging.

Using the same blog post from Activity 1, compose five different social media posts for *one* channel using interesting snippets from the content to serve as the post's five varying messages.

Chapter 9

Measuring and Analyzing Content

Why Measuring and Analyzing Content Is Important

Without taking a close look into the performance of your social media messaging, your content offers, or your advertising, you have no evidence that the content you've invested so much time producing is actually working.

There are three reasons that content and its performance should always be looked at with a keen eye. Measurement and analysis can help you:

1. Find out if your marketing efforts are driving the needle on sales.
2. Discover insights and determine where to go next.
3. Document and report on progress for future use cases.

THINK ABOUT THE POTENTIAL MONEY AND TIME YOU AND YOUR TEAM COULD BE WASTING ON CHANNELS THAT DON'T DRIVE YOU TOWARD MEETING YOUR GOALS
Analyzing your content helps close the loop on your day-to-day marketing efforts.

Thank you to Tori Zopf and Julie Kukesh for your contributions to this chapter.

Identifying success is all about analyzing your short-term efforts to eventually impact your end goals and long-term plan. But only 8% of marketers consider themselves successful at tracking the performance of their content marketing efforts.[1]

ANALYZING AND MEASURING YOUR CONTENT ALSO ALLOWS YOU TO UNCOVER INSIGHTS YOU MAY OTHERWISE HAVE MISSED

Do content offers in a certain format work for your business? Look for trends by channel, content format, and topic.

What works best for your audience? Has this changed over time?

Is there a new trend in your industry? Stay on top of it. Review not only your content but that of your competitors to be sure you're addressing basic questions and new developments.

LASTLY, MEASURING AND ANALYZING YOUR CONTENT MARKETING EFFORTS ALLOWS YOU TO DOCUMENT AND REPORT ON YOUR PROGRESS TO YOUR TEAM, MANAGERS, AND BEYOND

Are you progressing toward your goals in a timely fashion? Do you need to adjust your content plan, either because you're behind on your goals or way ahead? What insights did you gain from each of your marketing efforts? How can this be used to prove the value of the work you do or adjust next year's goals?

Given the amount of time you invest in creating content, it's essential to analyze the performance of the content to adjust your future content creation efforts and measure the results driven by your content to quantify the return on investment for the business.

How to Collect and Interpret Data

Content marketing can be hard to track. Unlike other areas of marketing, *it takes a lot of testing before you really discover something that resonates.* Often, content changes build up over time, which means when the results aren't immediate, it's easy to lose sight of why you're creating the content in the first place.

Stick to your goals and continue to track each campaign with the same zeal you had the first time around. Tracking data for the sake of tracking data isn't a valuable use of your time, but if you can derive actionable insights from data and adjust how you create content, you'll get that much closer to realizing a content formula that drives results and works best for your company and team.

There are six different areas to focus on when tracking and measuring your content marketing efforts:

1. Brand awareness
2. Engagement
3. Lead generation
4. Customer conversion and sales
5. Customer loyalty and retention
6. Website performance

Each area is based on different goals, and each drives different metrics.

First, Track Brand Awareness

Brand awareness can drive your company to the top of the search engine rankings and to the top of your potential customers' minds. But brand awareness means something different to everyone. Before digging in to measuring brand awareness, *be sure you and your team agree on which metrics and channels are important.*

In terms of metrics, where should you start? You could measure reach on various channels, including social media followers, external media coverage, or inbound links. You could also measure conversations about your brand, such as mentions in the press, social media, or reviews online. How many people are searching for your brand name and other branded keywords in search engines? Referral and direct traffic to your site may also be indicative of your audience's awareness of your brand as a trusted partner.

An effective way to track mentions of your brand online is to create a Google Alert for the name of your business. Google Alerts is a content change detection and notification service offered by Google.[2] The service sends emails to the user when it finds new results—such as web pages, newspaper articles, blogs, or scientific research—that match the user's search term(s).

Choose a few key metrics and stick to them. Although it can take a long time to drive the needle on brand awareness, if you stick to your SMART goals, you can measure incremental progress. As you may recall from Chapter 4, "Planning a Long-Term Content Strategy," SMART goals are specific, measurable, attainable, relevant, and timely.

Let's take a look at an example.

Margot is an experienced marketer responsible for content creation at her company. Margot's CEO asked her to quantify and measure her content marketing efforts as an overarching initiative for the year. From her experience, Margot knows there are six different key areas she can focus on to showcase content performance and analyze results, so she came up with a plan to run six content marketing measurement campaigns during the year, each targeted at measuring and analyzing content effectiveness.

In the past, Margot's CEO, board of directors, and vice president of public relations have all asked her to create initiatives that increase the company's brand awareness. For her first content marketing measurement campaign, she's going to focus on quantifying her content's impact on brand awareness. From her prior work, Margot knows that referrals from industry thought leaders play a big role in the way her sales team is able to close leads. So she chooses to focus her brand awareness efforts on increasing the number of thought leaders who are willing to recommend her company. Margot knows the importance of SMART goal setting, so she expands her goal: boost brand awareness in the first half of 2018 by increasing the number of recommending thought leaders from 3 to 10.

Margot should also be sure to nail down how and when she'll measure the number of referring thought leaders' inbound links as well as the plan for how she'll actually reach her goals. Will she be reaching out directly to thought leaders? Should she work through Twitter or other inbound efforts? Who are the people she and her boss would consider thought leaders? She should make a list and identify qualified thought leaders so she's not leaving it open to interpretation.

Second, Track Engagement

Measuring engagement will tell you not just who's seeing your content but who's interacting with it.

By measuring who's interacting with your content through engagements, you're interpreting feedback signals your readers are giving you without having to explicitly ask them how they like your content.

You can measure engagement on social media, including shares, likes, comments, and retweets. Are people sharing your posts to their own networks?

You can also measure engagement on owned channels, like your blog. Who's commenting on your blog, and how many comments does each post receive? Which blog posts and topics get the most comments? When you promote a content offer via email, do your recipients click and download the offer? Do they forward the email to a colleague or friend? After they download a content offer on a landing page, do people then share the landing page with their own networks? These engagement "signals" offer feedback that can help you determine the most popular and effective content pieces, topics, channels, and formats.

Engagement data not only helps you, the content creator, gain actionable insights into what content is working best, it can also help you tie engagement back to overall business goals.

In our example, Margot chose to run a second content marketing measurement campaign with a goal to increase the company's organic reach on Facebook by 150% by the end of 2018. To do so, she used content engagement metrics and data to showcase how content helped grow the organic reach on Facebook.

THIRD, TRACK LEAD GENERATION

This is an extremely important area for most content marketers. Using lead generation metrics, you can prove your time and your company's money is well spent.

Things you may consider measuring include how many leads you generate, and where they are in your funnel. Are they blog subscribers, or did they download a content offer? If so, which content offer?

Have you been able to qualify your leads, either through lead scoring or using lifecycle stages? Take a look at the number of marketing qualified leads, or MQLs, that represent leads that are making their way down your marketing funnel. Now look at the number of sales qualified leads, or SQLs, that reflect leads that are further down the funnel and more sales-ready. What is your ratio of MQLs to SQLs? If it's low, can you identify the gap?

What activities lead to someone becoming a lead? Can you attribute this conversion to a specific piece of content, campaign, or source? How much does it cost to acquire a lead? Or an MQL? An SQL?

Let's look back to our example. As you'll recall, Margot's CEO set an overarching initiative for the year, asking her to quantify and measure her content marketing efforts. In this third area of lead generation, Margot has an opportunity to really measure the impact of her content efforts on the business.

Margot's third content marketing measurement campaign is focused on using content for lead generation. She's measuring the impact of content pieces on the quality and quantity of leads generated by the end of 2018.

You can assess a lead's source through tracking URLs, which use simple tags at the end of a URL, also called UTM parameters. Through customized landing pages and tracking URLs, Margot can set up attribution reporting to tie her content pieces back to lead generation, and, eventually, the company's revenue stream. With tracking URLs, she can figure out which piece of content is generating the most qualified leads. From this insight, she can then continue to use that format over others.

You can create a URL with UTM parameters using Google's URL builder.[3] There are four areas to consider when building a URL with UTM parameters:

Website URL: Your website URL is where your visitors will land.

Campaign source: The campaign source helps you identify where your visitors are coming from, such as social media or a referral from a thought leader's website.

Campaign medium: Campaign medium is the type of content, such as an email or banner ad.

Campaign name: The campaign name is the title you give to your unique content or promotion.

After you provide all these components, Google will generate a URL for you to use in your promotional content. Create a new URL for every inbound link you want to track. Doing so will give you visibility into which specific link, and which piece of content, is generating traffic, leads, and sales.

If you're a HubSpot customer, you can also do this directly in HubSpot with the HubSpot tracking URL builder. And if your landing pages are created in HubSpot, your tracking URLs and attribution reporting is already taken care of.

An attribution report is used to understand every interaction a person makes with your business leading up to becoming a customer. This type of information makes clear when and why someone converted. In order for content marketers to be successful, they need to understand all of the engagements and actions that lead to valuable conversions throughout their funnel.

Margot could use attribution reporting to give individual content pieces the credit for a lead or sale.

Fourth, Track Customer Conversion and Sales

This is the real moneymaker. What's the return on investment (ROI) of your total content marketing efforts? Be sure to include creative and technical time, software costs, and overhead in your calculation of cost.

What's the cost of acquisition for a new customer? You can track the quality of sales influenced by content marketing in comparison to cold sales to help prove the ROI of your inbound and content marketing efforts. Do MQLs have a faster time to close than cold leads? Do they purchase more, and more often?

What's the ratio of leads to customers? By looking at this ratio in several different areas in the funnel, you can easily identify where your strategy may be falling short. Coordinate with your sales team to align your content marketing efforts with their selling process, and provide a smooth path for new prospects.

Margot may notice one of several things as she reviews her funnel. Based on what she learns in her data analysis, she decides to run her fourth content marketing measurement campaign to increase customer conversions by 10% by the end of 2018.

Margot's first observation from her analysis of her funnel is that although she now has 10 thought leaders driving traffic to the website, and although visits from referrals are up, referral traffic does not convert into customers.

Looking at an attribution report, Margot notices that 95% of her customers viewed her white paper on questions to ask during the sales process to ensure you're getting the best deal possible. Referral contacts skip the download in her nurturing campaign and go directly to the sales team. Margot decides that her campaign will include sending this white paper to referrals as well. She'll then be able to measure if the added touch point helps close the customer conversion gap for referral traffic.

Margot's second observation comes when she digs into her sales data and sees that referral contacts schedule initial meetings but don't move any further and rarely turn into customers. Margot decides to connect with her sales team to see if there's a disconnect once she hands off a lead. Can she create content to help her team at this point in the funnel?

FIFTH, TRACK CUSTOMER LOYALTY AND RETENTION

What's the lifetime value of a customer? Can you compare the lifetime value of a customer originally sourced by marketing to that of a sales-sourced customer?

How often do customers buy from you? Are they recommending your business to others? Do they come back for more?

Lifetime value and repeat business can be especially important for a company that has a high cost of acquisition and lower long-term cost to service. If you can get customers to stick with you over time, the return on your investment in closing them during the marketing qualification and sales processes grows exponentially.

In our example, Margot analyzes her company's current customer base to identify the segment of loyal customers with the best retention rates and the highest lifetime value. She designs her fifth content marketing measurement campaign to generate 15% more leads who match the profile of the current high-value segment customers to pass to sales each month by the end of 2018. She'll do this by promoting the handful of content pieces that all current high-value segment customers viewed before becoming a customer.

AND SIXTH, TRACK WEBSITE PERFORMANCE

What good is a content strategy if your website isn't optimized for user experience? Keep track of these key metrics to be sure your website makes it easy for customers to find and enjoy your content.

To measure your website's performance, you can look at traffic—including unique visitors and pageviews—and which sources of traffic are top performers for your business. If one channel drastically outperforms another, you may consider spending more money on that channel for increased ROI. Be sure to look at both the numerical value of traffic and also its worth to you—is traffic from your most popular source converting?

When it comes to organic search, pay attention to metrics for visits arriving from organic search to individual pages and the site overall. Make sure it's growing steadily over time. Search engines are becoming increasingly better at mimicking the human experience and our evaluation of what constitutes quality website content. In attempting to do so, they're looking at engagement with your website page to act as a proxy for votes of confidence for the quality of the page. High-quality website pages are thorough and complete and cover a topic comprehensively. Have you ever noticed that Wikipedia frequently shows up at the top of search results when you perform a search query? There are a number of factors that go into making this happen. One of those factors is that Google views Wikipedia content as high quality, because when you click through on that result and start reading the page content, you'll notice that it covers the topic in depth and discusses the who, what, why, where, and when of that topic.

For example, if you perform a search query on Abraham Lincoln, Wikipedia claims the number one spot on the search engine results page (see Figure 9.1).

When you click through to Wikipedia's page to learn more about Lincoln, there's a detailed biography available, from early career and militia service to religious and philosophical beliefs.

FIGURE 9.1

To measure your website's performance, you can also look at data for time on page and bounce rate with free tools like Google Analytics.

For her sixth content marketing measurement campaign, our marketer, Margot, is going to improve her website conversion rate of inbound traffic from search engines by 15% by the end of 2018.

Her content campaign for the first website performance goal of increasing visits is a twofold content strategy.

First, she'll select 10 website pages that are influential in driving sales, and she'll update the content on those pages to be high quality, comprehensive, and thorough, all with the intention to drive more engagement. She'll measure the increase in the number of visits, the search rank of the page, and the time on page over time to see if her content changes affected these metrics.

Second, Margot will write a series of blog posts around a certain topic to attempt to increase website traffic and generate more visits to the site from readers of those posts.

Margot's content campaign for measuring a page's influence on website conversion will focus on looking at the performance of the assets she's created. How does one landing page compare to another? Is one of her forms drastically out-converting the others? Through continuous monitoring and A/B testing, she intends to consistently improve her site's performance month over month with regards to conversion.

Now that we know what types of metrics you can record to measure your company's goals, it's time to look at how to report on and analyze that data.

What to Do with Data after You've Collected It

Once you've collected a set of data, it's important to review it with the key stakeholders at your company. This may include you, your team, and your management chain, all the way up to the C-level executives.

First, compare your results to the goals you set. Did you meet your goals? Why or why not? Use these new metrics to update your goals for the next month, quarter, or year.

Be sure to look for trends in content theme, format, promotion channels, and persona. Group your content into categories based on key similarities and try to draw some conclusions.

Telling the story of your data is one of the most important skills for a marketer to develop. It's not good enough to simply show the data; you must be able to convince your audience of its importance and relevance to company-wide goals and initiatives.

The First Step in Telling a Story with Data is to Identify Your Audience

Presenting to C-level executives or your management team is a much different scenario than speaking to the individual contributors on the marketing team. The stakes are different, and what they care about in terms of results is different as well. Think of the various internal stakeholders at your company. What would they appreciate hearing about when you speak to them about performance?

Have a Conversation with the Stakeholders at Your Company to Discuss What They're Looking for in Terms of Reporting

Ideally, *this conversation should take place before you run a campaign.* Why? You need to be sure you're set up to track the relevant metrics, and you need to be sure you're setting campaign SMART—specific, measurable, attainable, relevant, and timely—goals that align with the metrics the key stakeholders value.

Don't Just Look at the Numbers They Tell You to Look At

There may be other metrics you can use to support your story. After determining what your audience cares about, choose any additional key metrics—often referred to as key performance indicators or KPIs—that represent progress toward your audience's goals. Just like your goals, your reporting should be SMART.

Once You Have a Set of Metrics for Each Stakeholder or Type of Goal, Set Yourself up for Success by Building a Template or Dashboard That Tracks Each Metric

By building a template, you can easily export data and fill in the blanks at the required cadence without having to duplicate your efforts each month. A dashboard makes it even easier to track your progress by compiling data automatically. HubSpot helps you create custom dashboards and automatically share them at any frequency you choose with members of your team.

You should plan to have a weekly recurring meeting with your marketing team to review each campaign's performance and make any changes necessary. It's important to adjust each campaign and content effort continually so that by the end of the campaign, you successfully hit your SMART goals.

You should set up less-frequent meetings with the key stakeholders of each campaign as well. Having a kickoff meeting, monthly progress updates, and a wrap-up meeting to communicate your progress toward KPIs should do the trick.

To see what this looks like in action, let's take a look back at our example.

If you recall, Margot is an experienced marketer responsible for content creation at her company. As an overarching initiative for the year, Margot's CEO asked her to quantify and measure her content marketing efforts.

From her experience, Margot knows there are six different key areas she can focus on to showcase content performance and analyze results. She develops a plan to run six content marketing measurement campaigns during the year, all with the intention to measure and analyze content effectiveness.

Margot first identifies the key stakeholders for each of the six content marketing measurement campaigns.

Next, she plans to have a kickoff meeting before launching each campaign with only the key stakeholders related to that campaign. For instance, for Margot's first campaign focusing on quantifying her content's impact on brand awareness, she sets up one meeting with her CEO and a second meeting with both the board of directors and vice president of PR. Since brand awareness is important to both stakeholder groups, she brings them all into the conversation. However, she holds separate meetings because the CEO has different brand awareness priorities.

During each key stakeholder kickoff meeting, Margot starts by confirming that these key stakeholders are interested in receiving her campaign support, later confirming the campaign SMART goals together. She guides the discussion by offering some suggestions for the types of metrics available for that type of campaign, and together they identify relevant metrics to track. She wraps up the meeting by discussing what types of reporting the key stakeholders would find valuable, making sure to specify frequency and format. She always recommends meeting in person to deliver the agreed upon reporting, and she typically suggests making it a brief, 10-minute add-on agenda item to their regular recurring meeting. Last, she makes sure to set up a dedicated midpoint review meeting and wrap-up discussion where the campaign is the sole agenda item with these key stakeholders. Margot always follows up these in-person reporting meetings with a report and/or presentation. She does this via email or on a shared workspace to memorialize the work she's done and the progress she's made toward their agreed upon goals.

Using the process outlined earlier you can determine which metrics are important to track based on your content marketing goals and set yourself up to track each one. By looking closely at the metrics you, your team, and other stakeholders care about, you can present a coherent case for the time and money you spend on content creation and promotion while also making recommendations for where to expand.

Remember, your marketing is only as good as your results.

Chapter 9 Homework

Activity 1

It's important to properly track the performance of your SMART goals and keep key stakeholders in the loop.

List the name and position of key stakeholders who should stay informed of your content marketing efforts. Not every stakeholder is created equal. Some prefer granular details while others want high-level progress updates.

List the communication cadence for each key stakeholder as well as their preferred format of communication (i.e., detailed report vs. short email).

Activity 2

Save yourself hours of time by using a reporting template that matches your key stakeholders' needs.

Read this article and use a Google Sheet to create a reporting template (or two): bit.ly/2f9JZpK.

Chapter 10

Developing a Growth Marketing Mentality

What Is Growth Marketing?

First and foremost, let's define what growth marketing is. Growth marketing is a blend of marketing, sales, customer success, support, and any other division or operation within your organization. It's an integrated approach to growing your business and optimizing your content marketing efforts through constant testing across marketing channels. The goal of a growth marketer is to identify new opportunities that will help build and engage your organization's audience.

This approach is important for content marketers, as it can help them find new ways to communicate with their audience, whether it is via a new marketing channel or a piece of content to test.

We're in an age where new channels of communication are frequently surfacing in the online marketing space. Channels like Facebook, Twitter, Instagram, Pinterest, Snapchat, Messenger, and so on are becoming dominant channels for sources of information.

What's even better about these channels is that each has its own advertising platform, making it easy to expand the reach of

---

Thank you to Sujan Patel for your contribution to this chapter.

157

your top-performing content. Social media ad spend will likely exceed $35 billion in 2017, yet it only accounts for 13.9% of the total digital ad spend.[1]

The old-school digital marketing players—like search engine optimization (SEO), PPC, display, retargeting, and email marketing—are still important, but they've become increasingly more crowded and it's hard to stand out. As time goes on, these players will become more competitive and expensive, meaning the return on investment (ROI) is becoming less and less valuable.

Take a look at SEO. SEO is only a little over a decade old, but it's crowded. Google receives over 90,000 search queries every second from people who are searching for answers to problems they're trying to solve.[2] And there's so much content out there that Google has evolved their algorithm to require more than just doing SEO to do SEO.

That being said, if you can integrate these new channels into your existing efforts, like blogging, SEO, and paid media, then you're going to give yourself the best chance at achieving success.

A growth marketing approach will require you to manage more pieces, more people, and more integration between departments. But when everything bands together, it can work well.

How Can You Develop a Growth Marketing Mindset?

There are three things you need to develop a growth marketing mindset within your organization:

1. You need to understand your marketing funnel.
2. You need to have a framework to properly operate and improve your marketing funnel.
3. You need to get buy-in on instilling a growth mindset in the rest of your organization.

First, You Need to Understand Your Marketing Funnel

Before you do anything, you need to understand what you're working with. That's why it's important to identify and understand your marketing funnel.

Just like the buyer's journey, there are three stages to every marketing funnel (aka the marketing machine which we reviewed earlier):

1. The top of the funnel, which is generally the awareness stage.
2. The middle of the funnel, which encompasses the consideration stage.
3. The bottom of the funnel, which is typically the decision or conversion stage.

These stages of your funnel can differ by industry and company, so it's important to understand what they mean to you.

Once you identify your marketing funnel, *start putting metrics next to each stage, and be realistic.*

Metrics you might want to focus on include traffic, marketing qualified leads, marketing qualified leads to sales qualified leads, conversion rates, cost to acquire a customer, repeat customer rate, and month-over-month and year-over-year growth.

Whatever metrics you end up tracking, you need to understand the data. *Being able to quantify your metrics will help you find your strengths and weaknesses within your funnel.*

Once you quantify your metrics, start looking for weaknesses within your funnel. They may stem from other parts of your organization, but for the time being, all you really need to know is what they are and where they sit in your funnel.

Some businesses may have a weak funnel, one with a bottleneck when converting visitors to trials. Some businesses might not be able to get their trials to convert into customers.

Others may get conversions, turning their leads into customers, but they never talk to their customers and turn them into referrals.

Most businesses face one of two weaknesses in their marketing funnels.

The first weakness is the top of the funnel, where there isn't enough traffic coming to the website to make any type of conversion. Not just a sale, but any type of conversion, like an email opt-in, starting a trial, downloading a content offer, and so on.

The second weakness is conversion rate, or lack thereof. You may be getting people to your site, but they're not converting or doing what you want them to do.

After you identify your weaknesses, you'll want to find your marketing funnel's strengths. Which channels are your business's top revenue producers?

Now That You Understand Your Funnel, You Can Move On to Identify a Framework to Properly Operate and Improve Your Marketing Funnel

You're going to identify a framework using the bull's-eye framework shown in Figure 10.1.

The bull's-eye framework is a structured three-step approach to gaining traction. With so many different channels out there, understanding where to start can be difficult. *The bull's-eye framework will help you organize your channels and identify which ones help you create traction.*

Let's review each ring of the bull's-eye framework.

- The *center ring* holds your top three performing channels. These are the channels that have the highest potential of gaining traction for your business.
- The *middle ring* holds your secondary channels. These may not be your top performing channels, but they have

the potential to gain traction. These are your possibility channels.

♦ And lastly, the *outer ring* holds your long-shot channels. These channels may not be something on your radar, but it's important to list them out.

Once you've identified your channels, start running a series of tests. Each test should be geared toward uncovering how much it'll cost to acquire a customer through a specific channel, how many customers are available through this channel, and whether there are customers in this channel who you want to work with.

There are two phases to this process: ideation, and planning and implementation. Don't do these two things together, as they require the use of different parts of your brain. The left side of your brain will focus on planning and implementation, with items like determining the impact of the tests, ROI, and the resources needed to complete the tests. The right side of your brain will focus on ideas and creativity to help solve your problems.

Start with ideation. Brainstorm ideas on how you could use this channel for traction. For example, if you were to attend a

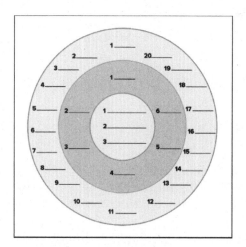

Figure 10.1

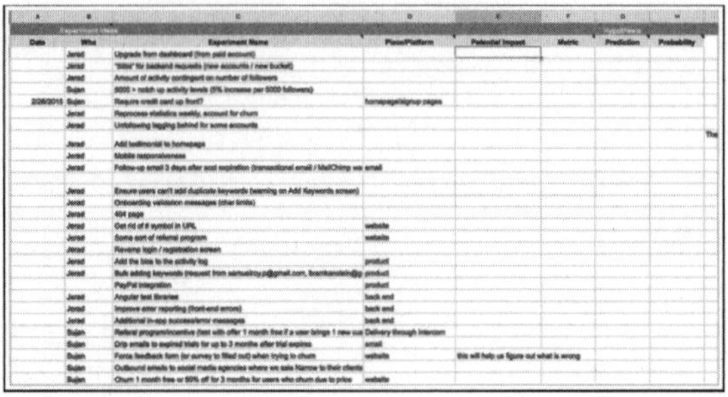

FIGURE 10.2

conference, which conference would it be? Or if you were to generate a partnership with an influencer, who would that be with? Most people will skip this step, but take the time to think of at least one idea per channel.

To help organize your ideas, use something like Google Sheets. Figure 10.2 illustrates an example of a spreadsheet that growth marketer and entrepreneur Sujan Patel uses to organize his ideas.

You'll notice he has columns to help organize his thoughts, such as:

- Date
- Who's in charge of the experiment
- Experiment name, the platform
- Potential impact
- Metric
- Prediction
- Probability

This is an effective, simple way to get experimental thoughts out of your head and into a document.

Not all ideas will work. In fact, most will fail, and that's okay. Each test is meant to prove or disprove your hypothesis with real answers. But don't sell your ideas short; write them down if you think they have the potential to gain traction.

Once you make a list of ideas, leave it. Give yourself a few days to reflect on them. You want the right side of your brain to shut off so the left side of your brain can kick into gear. This way, you can look at it from a different perspective and start thinking about implementing next steps, resources needed, and so on.

If the tests go the way you hope, you should produce positive results. This is when you should start focusing your efforts on your most promising channels.

Again, *the goal of this testing is constant optimization of your channels.* You want to make sure you exhaust all of your options, wringing out as much value from your channels as possible.

THE LAST STEP IS TO DEVELOP A GROWTH MARKETING MINDSET WITHIN YOUR ORGANIZATION

It's important to get the rest of your organization involved. You need to get them addicted to and excited about the idea of growth.

And although every department is important, there are three departments you should focus on first: customer service, support, and success; the sales team; and the team that manages your organization's products and services. Not all companies have these departments, or they might have one person managing multiple departments. And in that case, make note of the suggestions for each department and apply them to your specific organizational structure.

Let's start with the customer service, support, and success team. These folks are on the front lines with your customers after the transaction is made. They know the struggles and pain points of your customers. This team should always be searching for the customer's problems and identifying how their experience can be improved.

To do this effectively, there needs to be an open communication channel for this group to engage with customers. Whether it's social media, email, or phone, make it easy for customers to understand how to reach out when they need help.

Once you know the problems and pain points of your customers, you can start creating content that solves their needs, and scale it rather than reinventing the wheel for each new problem that arises.

Remember, *while customers may love your product or service, they're going to really love the content you produce if it's helpful to them.*

Also, don't just focus on the pain points and problems; make sure to capture the successes and wins for your customers. Knowing these will help you create valuable testimonials for your organization that you can share with everyone on your website, social media channels, and so on.

The next department to focus on is the sales team. The sales team is actively talking to prospects before they either become customers or decide not to do business with you. And because your sales team is engaging with prospects frequently, they have a good idea of why prospects convert into customers, why they don't, possible resources needed to help the sales process, and, most importantly, why not all buyer personas are created equal.

For example, maybe a small business prospect needs an email once per week because more than that would be too much communication. On the flip side, an enterprise-level customer may need more frequent emails per week to help with the long buying cycle. It's valuable information like this that allows you to better target and customize the content experiences for your customers and prospects. It's never a one-size-fits-all approach.

Also, the sales team will have insight into why prospects turn into customers. Maybe there's something said before the deal closes, such as a promise or guarantee. This could be great copy that should be incorporated into your marketing and website content.

And last, you'll want to focus on the team that's in charge of your organization's products and services. Get buy-in from the members who are in charge of your products and services. It's important to use logic and respect when explaining why customer buy-in is key. The best place to start is with the leader of the group.

When explaining why a growth marketing mindset is important, use feedback from the customer service, support, and success team to influence what your organization's customers want more of. This way, your organization can focus on growing based on what your customers want, not just what you think they want.

Once you instill this mindset into your organization, it can become a regular routine, like eating breakfast.

To recap, you need to know your marketing funnel, you need to have a framework to properly operate and improve your funnel, and you need to get buy-in on instilling a growth mindset within your organization.

What Are Some Growth Marketing Pro Tips?

There are hundreds of things you can do to improve the top, middle, and bottom of your funnel, but let's talk about proven tactics. Remember, growth is a mindset, and it's all about execution. You can have the best strategy or tactics in the world, but without execution, they mean nothing.

With that said, let's jump straight in by starting with the top-of-the-funnel tactics.

THE FIRST TOP-OF-THE-FUNNEL TACTIC IS FACEBOOK ADS

Facebook is a great way to target prospects because you can create custom audiences and get your content in front of relevant prospects.

For example, if you know your customers are between the ages of 30 and 40, own cats, and purchase from sites like

Amazon, you can create an audience that targets people with these specific traits.

As part of creating a custom audience, Facebook allows you to upload an email list of people you want to reach. Facebook will then look for their Facebook accounts using the associated emails you uploaded. This is a great way to stay in front of your audience without sending them an email.

There are two ways Facebook custom audiences help to grow your top-of-the-funnel reach:

1. Launching targeted ads.
2. Growing a relevant audience with a look-alike campaign.

Let's start with launching targeted ads.   Facebook ads are a great way to get your content in front of your audience. You can create ads for your most successful content, helpful videos, and your latest blog posts.

This will help nurture your audience. You might have emailed your users the same content, but when users discover content on their own—such as finding it in their Facebook newsfeed—they perceive you as more authoritative in your industry.

The second way to use Facebook custom audiences is to create a look-alike campaign to match 1% to 2% of your target demographic.   By setting your custom audience to match 1 to 2%, you're ensuring your look-alike audience closely resembles your persona. This is a great way to target new prospects based on similarities with your existing customers, rather than based on keywords they're searching for on Google AdWords.

ANOTHER TOP-OF-THE-FUNNEL TACTIC IS SECONDARY SEO

Secondary SEO involves being included or referenced on top websites that already rank well on search engines, like Google, for a particular keyword.

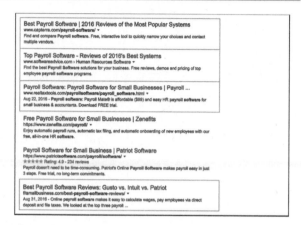

FIGURE 10.3

It can take weeks, months, or even years to increase your Google rankings. The shortcut is being referenced on sites that already rank well. Let's check out a few examples.

In the example shown in Figure 10.3, the keyword "payroll software" generates a search engine results page with four different review websites.

If you want traffic from a high-volume keyword like this that could be hard to rank for, all you have to do is get listed on one or more of the four websites outlined with a box on this page in Figure 10.3. Often it's as simple as submitting your company and getting a few reviews.

Let's check out another example, shown in Figure 10.4.

The keyword "growth hacking" generates a search engine results page with the question-and-answer website Quora showing up in the seventh position.

If you were the top answer on that particular question, you'd receive traffic from that high-volume search term. Sujan Patel did exactly that two years ago when he launched his growth marketing e-book, *100 Days of Growth*. This resulted in hundreds of visitors a month, which boosted sales of his

FIGURE 10.4

ebook. In total, *Quora was the third-highest traffic and sales driver for his ebook.*

All right, let's move on to the middle- and bottom-of-the-funnel tactics.

FIRST, USE YOUR BLOG CONTENT TO NURTURE YOUR NEW TRIALS OR CUSTOMERS

You can use your blog content and all of your content marketing efforts not just for the top of the funnel but also to guide potential customers through the middle and bottom of your funnel. All you need to do is take your best or most helpful content and include it in the onboarding emails your trial and new users receive.

NEXT, ADD URGENCY THROUGH DEADLINES, LIMITED QUANTITY, OR TIMING

Creating a sense of urgency is a great way to encourage people to take action. For example, make offers available for less than 24 hours. Creating a bottleneck forces the potential client to make a decision.

On to the Final Tactic: Concierge Onboarding

Concierge onboarding is a method for guiding your potential customers through purchasing your product or service. Often, when scaling your marketing efforts, you lose touch with identifying friction points that keep prospects from becoming customers. Concierge onboarding forces you to talk to your customers, learn what those pain points are, and address them on the spot. From there, you can apply your learnings to the onboarding content or update content on your website.

Concierge onboarding works well for new companies or established companies trying to scale a channel—what works when you have 100 new customers compared to 5,000 new customers will change. The friction points will change. *Talking to your customers will help you understand these issues immediately.*

And there you have it: All the information you need to become a growth marketer. But remember, digital media is an ever-evolving landscape. New opportunities will emerge and current platforms will change, so make sure you're ready and open to new possibilities you can use before your competitors do.

Chapter 10 Homework

Activity 1

Before running your next marketing test, you first need to identify your business's marketing channels.

This way you can organize your initiatives based on importance by channel.

Organize your marketing channels by writing out these bull's-eye framework fields in a Google Doc or Sheet:

1. **Identify your business's inner ring**—These are your three top-performing marketing channels that account for the majority of your business revenue.
2. **Identify your business's middle ring**—These are your six secondary marketing channels that help drive business revenue, but are not as effective as the inner-ring marketing channels.
3. **Identify your business's outer ring**—These are your marketing channels that are the least helpful with driving business revenue. This ring includes marketing channels you're currently active on as well as marketing channels you've yet to become a member of. That being said, it is important to identify as many relevant marketing channels as possible for your business.

Activity 2

Boost your awareness online through secondary SEO.

Go to Quora.com and find a question that's relevant to your business or industry. Provide a thoughtful response, while trying to engage with others in the thread.

Pro tip: If it makes sense and provides value, consider inserting a link to a relevant resource on your website.

Chapter 11

Creating Topic Clusters and Pillar Pages

Why Are Topic Clusters Important?

Content marketers are constantly battling for the attention of their audience. But with all the content being published online, search engines like Google are being forced to better organize and showcase the content they think would be helpful to the searcher. This led Google to release a zoo of updates over the years.

The first notable update, which really shook things up, was Google's "Hummingbird" algorithm update in 2013.[1] This update focused on parsing out phrases rather than focusing on specific search queries. Many search engine optimizers and content marketers viewed this as an initial shift from a keyword to topic focus in regards to content creation and website organization.

The next major update happened in 2015—Google's Rank-Brain algorithm update.[2] RankBrain is Google's machine-learning artificial intelligence system that interprets people's searches to find pages that might not have the exact words they searched for. Google is able to do this by associating past search history with similar themes and pulling together keywords and phrases to provide a better context-driven search engine results page.

Thank you to Ken Mafli for your contribution to this chapter.

All this change brings opportunity for content marketers to be found and, more important, be found by their ideal audience. That's a key facet to creating successful content in today's online environment. Most forget it's not just about creating content for the search engine. Search engines aren't the ones filling out the forms on your website. Search engines aren't the ones sharing your content on social media. *Search engines aren't your customers; humans are.*

If you want to create effective content that converts visitors into leads and eventually customers, you need to create a helpful, positive user experience that solves for both the searcher and the search engine, not just one or the other.

Here's how your content can solve for both: Create targeted clusters of relevant content that each covers a specific core topic in depth. These targeted clusters then need to lead to a centralized hub, known as a content pillar.

What is a content pillar? A content pillar (also known as a pillar page) is a website page that covers a broad topic in depth and is linked to form a cluster of related content.

How Do You Create an Effective Topic Cluster and Pillar Page?

Let's review the relationship between a topic cluster and a pillar page.

First, You Need a Core Topic

This should be something broad, usually two to three words—something that can be dug into and explained on a deep level.

Sales qualification is a great example of a core topic (see Figure 11.1).

Your core topic will take the shape of your pillar page; *your core topic will be what you're trying to rank for on search engines.*

FIGURE 11.1

Next, Identify Your Topic Cluster, Which Will be Made up of Several Relevant Subtopics

A subtopic should be strong enough to stand alone—in the form of a blog post or video—but when combined with other like-themed subtopics, it should be relevant to and support your core topic.

In this case, "What is a qualified prospect?" and "What is BANT?" are examples of strong subtopics that support the core topic of sales qualification.

And What Completes This Content Pillar, Which Solves for Both the Searcher and the Search Engine, is Connecting Everything through a Series of Hyperlinks

By linking all relevant subtopics to the core topic (i.e., pillar page), you're funneling all of your traffic to the main resource hub on this topic.

Let's see this in action (Figure 11.2).

If you performed a Google search for sales qualification, this is what the first page listing would look like.

At the top, you'll see Google generated a featured snippet, which is the search engine's way of answering your question simply without you having to click through to the page. In this case, Google assumes that if you're looking for information on "sales qualification," then you'll find value in the BANT qualification framework—information that's pulled from a HubSpot resource called "The Ultimate Guide to Sales Qualification."

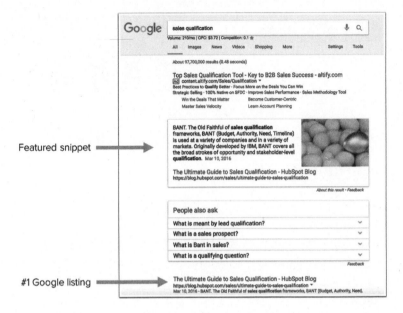

Featured snippet ➤

#1 Google listing ➤

FIGURE 11.2

Below the featured snippet you'll see HubSpot also claims the number one listing for "sales qualification" with the same resource, "The Ultimate Guide to Sales Qualification."

In a world of trying to rank for broad terms, this is what you're striving for: The featured snippet as well as the number one ranking. It's also worth noting, that the average first page ranking will also rank well for about 1,000 other relevant keywords.[3] So, optimizing for one topic can result in many different rankings on search engines.

Let's say you're interested in learning more about the BANT qualification framework, so you click the link in the search result to learn more. You'd be taken to the page shown in Figure 11.3.

After the first few paragraphs, you'll see a table of contents that lets you know you can navigate through the guide by clicking each section. Each section title has an anchor link attached to it, which, when clicked, will take you to the specific section on the page where it explains that topic in depth.

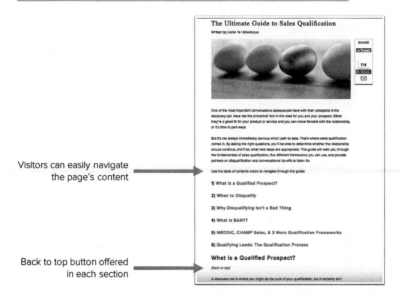

Visitors can easily navigate the page's content →

Back to top button offered in each section →

FIGURE 11.3

You'll also notice a "Back to top" button. This feature is a must-have for a good user experience on a page of this length, as it allows the reader to jump back to the top after reading a specific section. The last thing you want is your reader having to scroll back up through a long-form content page to get to the top.

Going back to our example, you found yourself on this page because you clicked through to learn more about the BANT qualification framework, which is number four on "The Ultimate Guide to Sales Qualification."

By clicking the anchor link, you're taken to the specific portion on the page that discusses the BANT qualification framework in depth (see Figure 11.4).

And within this section, you'll notice there's a link on "average of 5.4 people to make a buying decision." When clicked, it takes you to another HubSpot resource titled "Why Custom Positioning Isn't Enough to Close Deals Anymore." This is another relevant subtopic that supports sales qualification.

Not every relevant subtopic you have will be referenced on the pillar page (and that's okay). That's because you may have

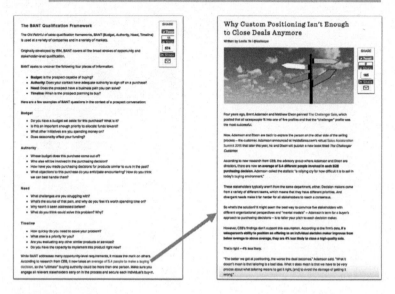

hundreds, even thousands, of subtopic pages that support your core topic. Instead, you can strategically link to relevant subtopic content throughout your pillar page when it makes sense and when it provides value to the website visitor. Just make sure all relevant subtopic pages connect to the pillar page. Remember, keep the user experience and the story you're trying to tell in mind.

So that's how this page solved for the searcher by offering a positive user experience, but how did this page solve for the search engines in terms of traffic and visibility?

This page receives more than 1,500 organic, nonpaid visits from search engines per month.

So how do you create a pillar page?

First, let's review the two most widely used pillar-page formats:

1. Resource pillar page
2. 10x content pillar page

LET'S START WITH THE RESOURCE PILLAR PAGE

The resource pillar page focuses on internal and external links. The goal of this pillar page is to be a helpful resource in connecting the reader with the most relevant sources on a specific topic (even if it means sending people off your site).

For example, take a look at the pillar page shown in Figure 11.5, Help Scout, a simple customer service software company, created on "customer acquisition."

This resource pillar page is composed of multiple sections that offer links to internal and external resources.

Generally, you wouldn't want to send people away from your website, but this approach is solving for the visitor, not your business.

The biggest advantage of a pillar page format like this is you have the opportunity to generate inbound links from sources

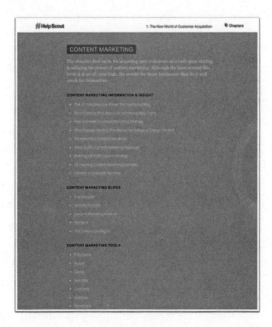

FIGURE 11.5

you include on the page. This page has hundreds of inbound links, most of which are sources mentioned on the page.[4]

For this type of page, you'll need to develop an outreach plan to let the sources know the page exists.

Next Is the 10x Content Pillar Page

The goal of this type of pillar page is the same: to provide a comprehensive overview of a specific topic. But the 10x pillar page is generally made up of your owned media (content assets you can control and manage). The format of this page is similar to that of an ungated ebook or a guide.

Yes, I said ungated content. *Ungating thought leadership content in the Awareness stage helps solve for both the search engine and the website visitor, not one or the other.* It solves for the search engines because they're able to recognize the clustering of like-themed content on a specific subject, and it solves for the website visitors because it gives them the opportunity to view your content before deciding to commit to downloading it.

The trick is making the 10x content pillar page conversion-focused by packaging the page's content into a downloadable resource.

You may be asking yourself, why the heck would anyone give you their elusive email address if they can view the same content on a website page without providing any identifying information?

Well, HubSpot did a study in March 2017, and we found that 90% of website visitors prefer to read our lengthy content in a PDF as opposed to on a website page. But this preference is not limited to HubSpot's content. *It's human nature to want to take something with you if you find value in it.*

Think of it this way: Let's say you go to a bookstore looking for a new book to read. You'd probably wander up and down the aisles, flipping through pages of various books until you find one that meets your needs. Once you find a book you enjoy, you'll probably go to the checkout counter and buy it to take it with you, as opposed to staying in the bookstore hour after hour and day after day, reading this piece of content.

This is the experience you're trying to replicate, but it can only be done if your content provides value to the reader. We've reached an age where everyone seems to have an ebook or guide, but the quality of that content is a different story. Sure, you may be getting leads, but what if people don't find value in your content? They most likely won't continue building a relationship with you, so that lead you captured won't be as valuable as you think.

In contrast, the people who can view your content before downloading it and who then choose to fill out your form will be much more qualified because they're willingly giving you their information even though they've already seen what your content has to offer.

For example, take a look at the 10x content pillar page shown in Figure 11.6 on "email outreach" created by Mailshake, a simple cold email outreach tool.

FIGURE **11.6**

FIGURE **11.7**

This 10x content pillar page covers a comprehensive approach to email outreach with sectioned content.

Let's say you want to learn more about what an effective outreach email looks like. Click section three at the bottom of the page in Figure 11.6, "Examples of good (and great) outreach emails and what we can learn from them," and the link will direct you to that specific section on the page to learn more about it.

If you click a link in the table of contents at the top, you'll notice Mailshake offers the content as a packaged downloadable resource at the bottom of the page shown in Figure 11.7.

This way, if the visitor finds value in the content, they can choose to take it with them.

How well is this page performing? Well, in less than a year, this page has:

- Been viewed over 43,000 times
- Been shared on social media 398 times
- Attracted 372 inbound links
- Acquired 5,321 email opt-ins
- Acquired 402 customers

Let's review how a company called Etuma created their business's first ungated 10x content pillar page. Etuma helps transform unstructured text data into decision-making information for a business.

Although there's more than one way to create a pillar page, here's a seven-step process that Etuma followed to create an initial 10x content pillar page and topic cluster for their business:

1. Choose a core topic.
2. Identify a topic cluster.
3. Create blog posts for subtopic content.
4. Repurpose subtopic content into a downloadable offer.
5. Deconstruct downloadable offer into a 10x content pillar page.
6. Link relevant content to 10x content pillar page.
7. Create a conversion path for people to access 10x content pillar page.

Let's review each step in depth.

First, Etuma Identified a Core Topic for Their 10x Content Pillar Page

Etuma performed research on keywords its primary buyer persona, Customer Experience Manager Maggie, might use when looking for information online. Etuma identified the broad term "text analysis" and decided on it as the core topic because it's an Awareness-stage subject that Maggie would search for and it's connected to a product or service they offer.

If you're going to take the time to create content that educates your audience, make sure it connects to, and supports, at least one of your products or services. If it doesn't, ask why you're creating it in the first place.

Second, Etuma Identified Their Topic Cluster

You may already have content created in support of your core topic. Instead of reinventing the wheel, identify current owned media that's relevant to your core topic.

In this case, Etuma already had four pages of text analysis-themed blog content and a series of YouTube videos.

And while it may be great that you have subtopic content already created, don't sell your business short. Brainstorm a list of as many subtopics as possible that bring value to your core topic that have yet to be published.

Once you make a comprehensive list of subtopics, narrow it down to six of the strongest subtopics that support your core topic and its pillar page. Remember, you can continue growing your pillar page, so having a list of subtopics already identified will help make that process easier. That comprehensive list you made is the content gift that keeps on giving.

THIRD, ETUMA CREATED BLOG POSTS FOR THEIR SUBTOPIC CONTENT

If you're like Etuma and you choose at least one subtopic that needs content created, you're going to need a way to bring it to life. Create a blog post first because there are various opportunities for repurposing it in the future.

Etuma needed content for their subtopic "categorization systems," so they created a blog post titled "How to Create a Customer Feedback Taxonomy."

Once Etuma created this blog post, they had a blog for each one of their subtopics they identified.

FOURTH, ETUMA REPURPOSED ITS SUBTOPIC CONTENT INTO A DOWNLOADABLE OFFER

Once you have all the content you need to create your pillar page, repurpose the subtopic content into a downloadable offer. Remember, the goal here is to use the content you have to put together a helpful story for the reader, which explains the core topic in-depth.

Create the content offer before the pillar page. This way, you'll be able to prepare a highly relevant conversion action (downloading the content offer) to have on the pillar page so your business can start generating leads as soon as the page is published.

Fifth, Etuma Deconstructed Its Downloadable Offer into a 10x Content Pillar Page

Etuma took the same content offered in their guide and formatted it to fit on a website page.

By now you should understand how important content is, but *design is sometimes forgotten, and it's just as important, if not more important, than the content on the page.* You want people to have a positive experience when they're reading your content.

Think about the last bad experience you had at a restaurant you visited. Did you go back?

To make sure your 10x content pillar page provides a positive experience, check out the 13 layout tips outlined on Etuma's example (see Figures 11.8 and 11.9).

Let's review each layout tip in more detail.

Starting at the top left of the example, with tips 1, 2, and 3, apply consistent on-page search engine optimization best practices, referencing the core topic in your page title, URL, and H1 tag.

One thing to consider is the URL structure. Although the link Etuma chose is not technically wrong, they could have

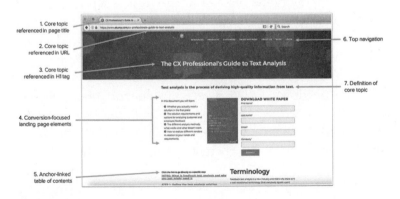

Figure 11.8

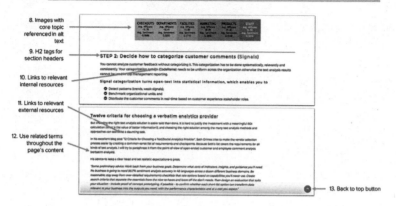

8. Images with core topic referenced in alt text

9. H2 tags for section headers

10. Links to relevant internal resources

11. Links to relevant external resources

12. Use related terms throughout the page's content

13. Back to top button

FIGURE 11.9

made the subfolder shorter and more broad, which would be more in line with the core topic (something like: https://www .etuma.com/text-analysis). Although this is a personal preference, shortening the subfolder helps account for future updates and modifications made to the page.

Moving down to tip 4, include conversion-focused landing page elements. Really, this is what a landing page should look like: text to the left with bullet points to describe the offer's value, an image of the offer's cover in the middle, and a form to fill out and access the offer to the right.

Insert the form directly on the 10x content pillar page. Doing so reduces the amount of conversion actions a reader needs to take to download the resource. That being said, if you're comfortable with a dedicated landing page with a form to access the offer, insert a call to action (CTA) on the pillar page to send readers there.

Moving down to tip 5, add an anchor-linked table of contents below the conversion point with the line "click the link to go directly to a specific section." This lets the visitor know they can view the content first before deciding to take it with them.

Moving up to the top right of the example and layout tip 6, you'll notice there's website navigation. The goal of this page is to create a positive experience for the visitor, not force them to convert as a landing page would.

Moving down to tip 7, there's a definition of the core topic. The core topic is defined at the top of the page, which helps optimize the page to be chosen as a featured snippet for that topic. A featured snippet is Google's way of trying to answer your search query simply without you having to click through to a page. It's the first thing people see before the search result listings.

Moving down to tip 8, use relevant images throughout the page, with the core topic referenced in the alt text. This helps optimize the images used on the page for image search results.

Moving down to tip 9, use H2 tags for section headers—don't even think about just increasing the text size and bolding it. Let's keep it simple, consistent, and neat. Using proper HTML structure helps provide a clean user experience and makes it simpler to update the page.

Moving down to tips 10 and 11, use relevant internal and external links to dig deeper into resources. Yes, I said external as well. It helps to use external links to validate your claims. Just use them strategically—for example, to support a claim or data point you need to reinforce.

Moving down to tip 12, reference your core topic throughout the page. But don't just repeat the exact phrase; search engines are smart enough to understand synonyms of your core topic phrase.

And finally, tip 13, have a "Back-to-top" button. This way, when people click a section they want to learn more about, they can easily jump back to the top. People probably won't read your entire page, but they may find one section interesting enough and want to download it and take it with them. You want to make this process as easy as possible for the visitor. Forgetting this step would require the reader to scroll endlessly, or it might feel like it, which could lead to frustration, which could lead to them leaving your page and going elsewhere.

Sixth, Etuma Linked Its Relevant Owned Media Content to Its 10x Content Pillar Page

Once you complete your 10x pillar page, you're going to need to hyperlink your subtopic content to it, creating your topic cluster.

The goal here is to connect all owned media that's relevant to the core topic to the pillar page using a hyperlink. The more content associated with your topic cluster and pillar page, the better.

And don't just add any old link text. Take the time to update the anchor text to something descriptive that supports the core topic (see Figure 11.10).

Etuma linked more than 20 relevant pieces of content to its 10x content pillar page. And you'll notice Etuma took the time to create descriptive anchor text to let the searcher and search engine know where they're going.

Seventh, Etuma Created a Conversion Path for People to Access Its 10x Content Pillar Page

The goal here is to let people know this content is available, because if you don't, you run the risk of a large portion of your

---

Text analysis generic or even industry specific Codeframe might not fulfill your granularity and reporting requirements. Make sure that either the vendor provides modifications to the Codeframe as a service or they give you an easy-to-use tool which you can use to tune the Topics.

Getting a lot of unstructured feedback from customers or employees? Looking for a way to analyze them? No worries, we wrote a "Guide for selecting the right method and tool for feedback analysis". Read it and you will be able to select the correct solution for your needs.

Topics: Feedback Analysis, feedback categorization, text analysis methods

Written by Matti Airas

My passion is to figure out how to turn open-text feedback into well structured usable information.

FIGURE 11.10

website visitors never finding it. Forgetting this step would be similar to building a new addition on your house without a door. No matter how great that room is, no one would be able to get in, so what's the point?

One placement to consider is to call out your pillar page in the top navigation on your home page through a one- or two-click process: one click if you offer it directly in the dropdown menu, two clicks if you have a resources page with multiple assets to organize and call out.

Etuma calls out their 10x content pillar page as a one-click option in their Resources tab (see Figure 11.11).

Another placement to consider is a dedicated section with a CTA near the top of the home page, with an image and descriptive supplemental text.

This doesn't mean it always needs to stay here on this page. You can promote the pillar page for a limited time, possibly for two weeks or a month, to support its publishing launch.

And there you have it: seven steps to creating an effective 10x content pillar page for your business.

FIGURE 11.11

Etuma has been creating content consistently for years, but this seven-step process helped the company make more sense of how to create, grow, and connect effective content.

But how well is it performing?

After two months, a member of Etuma's team said, "We're receiving about four times the leads (if you measure by quality) compared to before the text analysis content pillar."

Getting started tip: If you're looking for a place to start with creating topic clusters and pillar pages, consider deconstructing your existing Awareness- or Consideration-stage offers into 10x content pillar pages and offer the content as a packaged download.

I performed this exact experiment with Wild We Wander's DIY truck camper guide (see Figure 11.12).

You can see it here: wildwewander.com/diy-truck-camper.

The result? *In four months, our nonpaid, organic traffic coming from search engines increased 329%* (see Figure 11.13).

In an effort to better solve for the searcher and search engine, SmartBug Media decided to perform this experiment on

FIGURE 11.12

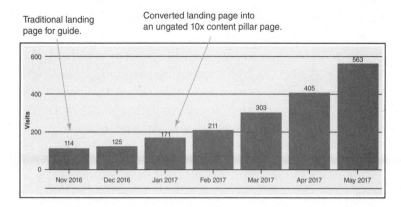

FIGURE **11.13**

their top-performing inbound marketing personas guide (see Figure 11.14).

You can see it here: smartbugmedia.com/inbound-marketing-personas.

In the first three months after publishing, Smartbug's 10x content pillar page received 4,800 views and over 1,000 downloads.

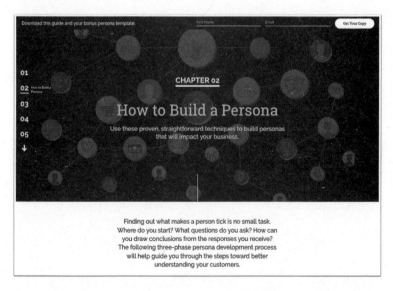

FIGURE **11.14**

Remember, if you have something valuable to say to your audience and the world, don't keep it locked up behind a form. Get it out there for all to see. Just make sure to package it in a way that makes it easy for people to take with them and enjoy elsewhere.

What's an Example of a Successful Pillar Page?

Your pillar page should always be under construction. You might need to make updates to keep it relevant or add new, fresh content to keep it performing at a high level. You need to maintain it. Otherwise, you're leaving yourself vulnerable for someone else to come in and outperform you—it happens all the time.

Let's check out a company that's taken the time to grow their topic clusters and pillar pages into the backbone of their content strategy: Townsend Security, a full-service data security provider.

You may remember this graph (Figure 11.15) from the introduction that showcases Townsend Security's nonpaid, organic traffic coming from search engines; the graph shows how their success was like a marathon, not a sprint, when it came to achieving results.

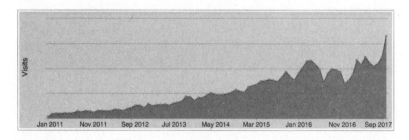

FIGURE 11.15

Well, Townsend Security's content marketing marathon training was fairly volatile in 2016, as you can see in the graph shown in Figure 11.15. Let's review this and learn what they did to overcome this hurdle.

Townsend started in 2016 with a positive lift in organic, nonpaid visits coming from search engines due to their content efforts. Townsend worked hard in 2015 with regular blogging, webinars, podcasts, white papers, and ebooks. The result: Townsend's traffic held steady in 2015, and in the first quarter of 2016, it had a robust rise in organic search visitors (27%).

But all that changed in the second quarter of 2016. Competition for its narrow band of keywords increased as new competitors entered the marketplace, and its larger rivals outspent them on online marketing. After a record high March and April, Townsend saw a 38% slippage in organic search visitors during the next three months (with a 28% slippage in one month alone). Townsend's hard work from the previous year evaporated. Although it fought back and did recoup some of that traffic, it still struggled to regain its high ground in organic searches.

In late September of 2016, Townsend's HubSpot Premier Inbound Consultant, Erin Sliney, introduced Townsend to the concept of creating a pillar page and topic cluster. So Townsend created a comprehensive 10x content pillar page around a broad topic. *The goal was to become the thought leader on "encryption key management."* And that's exactly what it did (see Figure 11.16).

During the editing process, Townsend wrote 20 social media updates and scheduled them to be published to their Twitter, Facebook, and LinkedIn accounts once the pillar page went live. Those updates were mixed in with Townsend's regularly scheduled social posts during the following eight weeks. Coupled with an email campaign promoting the pillar page to Townsend's active lead community, they were able to get the word out to those already familiar with the company.

FIGURE 11.16

FIGURE 11.16

To reach the wider community who might not yet know Townsend, the company inserted links to the pillar page by:

- Thoughtfully answering questions on Quora
- Adding insights to other blog posts through blog commenting
- Contributing thought leadership through guest posts published on other websites

And last, since Townsend had been blogging on encryption key management for years, it was easy to identify a topic cluster through a few dozen subtopic blog posts that were contextually similar. It could place internal links with descriptive anchor text on these posts pointing back to the pillar page. The links enhanced the reader's experience, since they were providing additional, relevant content for the reader to binge (as well as being a clear signal for search engines to understand what the pillar page was all about).

This shows how Townsend created and promoted their initial 10x content pillar page, but *how did they continue growing it to become the authoritative source on encryption key management?*

Townsend improved the on-page experience in four ways. They:

1. Offered various forms of media per section for the reader to engage with.
2. Sprinkled in relevant content offers that would help their buyer personas continue educating themselves through the buyer's journey.
3. Inserted a heat map on their pillar page to better understand performance and optimization next steps.
4. Connected relevant pillar pages through hyperlinks.

First, Townsend Offered Various Forms of Media per Section for the Reader to Engage With

To start, Townsend created graphics and optimized them for Google search results. To take it a step further, Townsend turned the images into interactive infographics with pop-up text using HTML5, which search engines can also read (see Figure 11.17).

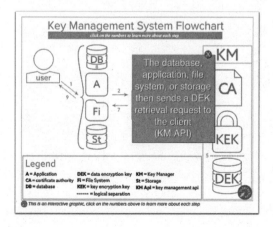

Figure 11.17

Next, Townsend repurposed various data points into infographic-like images (see Figure 11.18).

And last, Townsend repurposed content on the page into a video (see Figure 11.19), providing a quick overview of encryption key management. The video led to a 20% increase in average time on page.

Second, Townsend Sprinkled in Relevant Content Offers to Help Its Buyer Personas Continue Educating Themselves through the Buyer's Journey

Townsend offered additional content offers throughout the page based on relevancy, like a podcast (see Figure 11.20).

This is an effective way to help your visitors continue progressing through the buyer's journey—showing them what other content you have to offer when it makes sense.

We live in an age where people binge content. Platforms like Netflix promote this by releasing full seasons of a show at once, turning people into content-crazed couch potatoes.

Figure 11.18

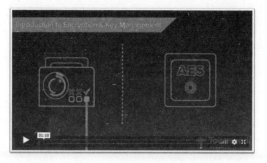

FIGURE 11.19

People want content now, and as much of it as they can consume until they're ready to make a decision, whatever that may be. The best thing you can do is find a way to keep people coming back to your content and continue to either educate or entertain them (or both). If you don't, someone else will.

Three months after publishing its 10x content pillar page and continually promoting it, Townsend had some interesting results:

- ◆ Organic, nonpaid traffic went up 55%.
- ◆ From all their marketing efforts combined, including social, PPC, and guest posting, March 2017 saw a record amount of total visitors to their website.
- ◆ *Of the people who visited the encryption key management pillar page, 63% decided to download it and take it with them.*

FIGURE 11.20

FIGURE 11.21

What about visibility on search engines? In August 2017, Townsend's 10x content pillar page claimed the number one position on Google for "encryption key management" (see Figure 11.21). It also shared the featured snippet with Wikipedia.

THIRD, TOWNSEND INSERTED A HEAT MAP ON ITS PILLAR PAGE TO BETTER UNDERSTAND PERFORMANCE AND OPTIMIZATION NEXT STEPS

Townsend's pillar page offers a lot of valuable content with multiple conversion actions. Because it wants to ensure its visitors are receiving the best content experience possible, Townsend used a heat map to see the engagement patterns on the page using Hotjar.

Hotjar is a new and easy way to truly understand your web and mobile site visitors' on-page experience.

For example, after placing a Hotjar heat map on its pillar page, Townsend learned that *people who visit the page are more*

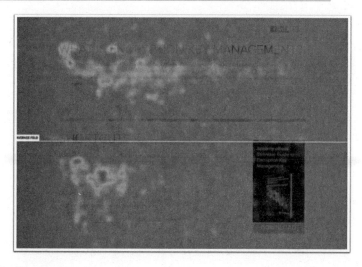

FIGURE 11.22

interested in learning about what encryption key management is before downloading the content in a packaged download. Here's a screenshot of Townsend's heat map at the top of their pillar page. Notice how all the engagement is happening around the CTA (see Figure 11.22).

But once visitors start clicking around to learn more about encryption key management, they're interested and willing to give their information in exchange for a packaged download of the content. *Interestingly enough, the CTA for the guide that's three-quarters of the way down the page led to the most conversions* (see Figure 11.23).

This information helped Townsend understand which sections people found the most value in that lead to conversions. It also showed Townsend that people prefer to peruse through the content before giving up their email address to download it and take it with them—*another effective data point to support Townsend's choice to ungate their content and offer it as a packaged download.*

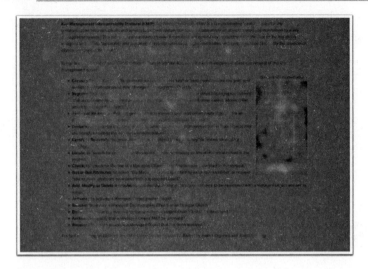

FIGURE 11.23

FOURTH, TOWNSEND CREATED ANOTHER 10X CONTENT PILLAR PAGE AND CONNECTED IT TO THE ENCRYPTION KEY MANAGEMENT PILLAR PAGE THROUGH A HYPERLINK

Results like this sparked a lot of interest at Townsend. They adopted the inbound methodology of marketing years ago, because it aligned with their heartbeat of being mentors, educators, and coaches first, and businesspeople second. Creating content through topic clusters, they feel, is a natural extension of that sentiment.

News traveled up to the CEO, who was so delighted by their results that he decided to create Townsend's next pillar page, "SQL server encryption."

Something important to note is that "SQL server encryption" is a subtopic of "encryption key management." You heard that right, a subtopic evolved into its own 10x content pillar page. That's the first step toward building a web of content and really going that extra mile to create a binge-worthy, positive user experience solves for both the search engine and website visitors.

What I love most about this example is how content creation has always been a major facet of Townsend's marketing plan. That being said, *the immense success Townsend received with topic clusters and pillar pages led to content marketing becoming a business-wide initiative that everyone rallied around.*

If your goal is to create content that attracts, converts, closes, and delights your ideal customers, then you need the commitment, excitement, and dedication of your entire company to make it happen.

Chapter 11 Homework

ACTIVITY 1

Select a guide or ebook that you've created, and deconstruct it into an ungated, conversion-focused 10x content pillar page.

Make sure the guide is Awareness-stage-focused but that it supports at least one or more of your products and services.

Figures 11.24 and 11.25 show two samples of 10x content pillar page layout tips to consider.

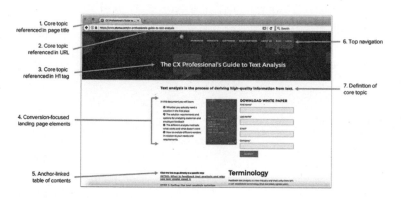

FIGURE 11.24

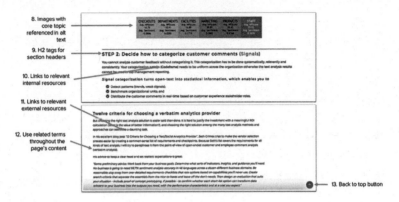

8. Images with core topic referenced in alt text

9. H2 tags for section headers

10. Links to relevant internal resources

11. Links to relevant external resources

12. Use related terms throughout the page's content

13. Back to top button

FIGURE 11.25

ACTIVITY 2

Attach a heat map to your 10x content pillar page. This way, you can easily see where people are engaging with your content, helping you determine optimization next steps.

1. Go to Hotjar (https://www.hotjar.com/) and create a free account.

2. Copy the JavaScript tracking to your site, and paste it into your tag manager or the <head> tag on every page where you wish to track visitors and collect feedback. (I recommend going the tag manager route so all your pages are accounted for.)

Chapter 12

The Results

Where to Go from Here

Congrats! By completing the chapters and activities in this book, you've taken the first step toward transforming yourself into an effective content marketer.

You're now ready to:

1. Start, manage, and grow a content process for your business.
2. Take the final Content Marketing Certification test to earn a valuable industry credential. Follow this link and click the "Take the Test" button: hubspot.com/cmc-exam.

The next step is to continue building and implementing your plan, staying consistent in your approach. Always be on the lookout for new content opportunities that have the potential to provide value to your audience. Remember, they're the reason you're doing this in the first place—if you want to start a relationship with your audience, give them the care and attention they deserve.

Want to continue your content marketing journey? We'd love to continue growing with you. Check out HubSpot Academy's content marketing training page: hubspot.com/content.

Let's transform the way the world does business, together. Remember to tweet me (@JustinRChampion) and HubSpot Academy (@HubSpotAcademy)—we'd love to hear from you and see what you and your business have achieved through your content marketing efforts. Plus, we're always looking for best-in-class work to showcase in HubSpot Academy training materials.

Always be learning,

Justin Champion | HubSpot Academy

Glossary

10-4-1 rule A ratio of how many messages to send over a 15-post period across your social media platforms.

A/B test A controlled experiment with two variants, A and B.

alt text A word or phrase that can be inserted as an attribute in an HTML document to tell website viewers the nature or contents of an image.

anchor link Visible, clickable text in a hyperlink.

Awareness stage When the buyer identifies there's a problem that's happening. This person performs research to learn more and find a possible solution.

blink test The commonly accepted three to five seconds during which a visitor lands on your website, judges it, and decides if they want to stay there and do something or abandon ship.

bull's-eye framework A structured three-step process on how companies can focus on the right channels for customer acquisition.

business-to-business (B2B) A type of transaction that exists between businesses, such as one involving a manufacturer and a wholesaler or a wholesaler and a retailer.

business-to-consumer (B2C) A type of transaction conducted directly between a company and consumers who are the end users of its products or services.

buyer persona A semifictional representation of your ideal customer based on quantitative and qualitative analysis.

buyer's journey The process a buyer goes through to become aware of, evaluate, and purchase a new product or service.

call to action (CTA) An image or line of text that prompts your visitors, leads, and customers to take action.

canonical tag A way of telling search engines that a specific URL represents the master copy of a page.

Consideration stage When the buyer has found one or more solutions to their problem. Now they're looking to find the solution that best meets their needs.

content management system (CMS) A software application or set of related programs that are used to create and manage digital content.

content marketing A strategic marketing and business process focused on creating and distributing valuable, relevant, and consistent content.

content pillar (aka pillar page) A website page that covers a broad topic in depth and is linked to from a cluster of related content.

Decision stage When the buyer is ready to make a well-informed decision, which is usually purchasing a specific product or service.

featured snippet A summary of an answer to a user's query, which is displayed above Google search results.

H tags Used to define HTML headings.

HTML (hypertext markup language) A standardized system for tagging text files to achieve font, color, graphic, and hyperlink effects on website pages.

HTML5 A markup language used for structuring and presenting content on the Internet. It's the fifth and current major version of the HTML standard.

inbound link A link from one site to another site.

inbound marketing A focus on attracting customers through relevant and helpful content and adding value at every stage in your customer's buying journey. With inbound marketing, potential customers find you through channels like blogs, search engines, and social media.

infographic A visual image, such as a chart or diagram, used to represent information or data.

keyword A word or phrase that's a topic of significance.

the marketing rule of seven A prospect needs to "hear" the advertiser's message at least seven times before they'll take action to buy that product or service.

noindex A tag that tells search engines not to include your page(s) in search results.

outbound marketing The traditional form of marketing where a company initiates the conversation and sends its message out to an audience.

return on investment (ROI) Usually expressed as a percentage and typically used for financial decisions, to compare a company's profitability, or to compare the efficiency of different investments.

search engine optimization (SEO) Techniques that help your website rank high in organic search results, making your website visible to people who are looking for your brand, product, or service via search engines like Google, Bing, and Yahoo.

search engine results page (SERP) The page displayed by a search engine in response to a query by a searcher. The main component of the SERP is the listing of results that's returned by the search engine in response to a keyword query. The page may also contain other results, such as advertisements.

topic cluster Enables deep coverage across a range of core topic areas while creating an efficient information architecture in the process.

UTM parameters Descriptive tags you add to a URL. When your link is clicked, the tags are sent back to Google Analytics and tracked.

Notes

Introduction: Your Content Marketing Transformation

1. John Deere's *The Furrow* has over 38,000 inbound links (https://majestic
.com/reports/site-explorer?q=https%3A%2F%2Fwww.johndeerefurrow.com
%2F&oq=https%3A%2F%2Fwww.johndeerefurrow.com%2F&IndexData
Source=F).
2. Although content marketing costs 62% less than outbound marketing, it generates more than three times as many leads (http://contentmarketinginstitute
.com/2016/08/content-marketing-stats/).

Chapter 1. Building a Content Creation Framework

1. HubSpot Blog Ideas Generator: A HubSpot tool that helps brainstorm blog
post ideas (http://hubspot.com/blog-topic-generator).
2. The average site visitor spends about three to five seconds scanning a
website before deciding to spend time looking through it (https://blog
.hubspot.com/blog/tabid/6307/bid/34061/How-to-Make-Sure-Your-
Website-Passes-the-Dreaded-Blink-Test.aspx).
3. Google Analytics: A free web analytics service offered by Google that
tracks and reports website traffic (https://analytics.google.com).
4. HubSpot: A company that offers marketing, sales, and CRM software that helps you
grow your business by generate leads and revenue (https://www.hubspot.com/).
5. Google Drive: A file storage and collaboration service developed by
Google (https://drive.google.com).

Chapter 2. The Power of Storytelling

1. The average adult spends more than 20 hours per week with digital media
(https://www.ofcom.org.uk/about-ofcom/latest/media/media-releases/
2015/time-spent-online-doubles-in-a-decade).

2. Google processes more than 5.4 million searches per minute (http://searchengineland.com/google-now-handles-2-999-trillion-searches-per-year-250247).

Chapter 3. Generating Content Ideas

1. James Webb Young, *A Technique for Producing Ideas* (New York: McGraw-Hill, 2003). Available at Amazon.com: (https://www.amazon.com/Technique-Producing-Advertising-Classics-Paperback/dp/B00ZT0R1BW/ref=sr_1_3?ie=UTF8&qid=1500586876&sr=8-3&keywords=james+webb+young+ideas).

2. Buzzsumo: A powerful online tool that allows any user to find out what content is popular by topic or by website (http://www.buzzsumo.com).

3. Quora: A question-and-answer site where questions are asked, answered, edited, and organized by its community of users (https://www.quora.com/).

4. Google Search Console (previously Google Webmaster Tools): A free web service by Google for webmasters. It allows webmasters to check indexing status and optimize visibility of their websites (https://www.google.com/webmasters/).

5. The first two positions in Google search results account for 51% of search traffic (https://searchenginewatch.com/sew/study/2276184/no-1-position-in-google-gets-33-of-search-traffic-study).

6. Venngage: An easy-to-use website where the most design-inept can create stylish content for websites, presentations, ads, social media, and much more (https://venngage.com/).

7. 90% of information transmitted to the brain is visual (https://blog.hubspot.com/blog/tabid/6307/bid/33423/19-reasons-you-should-include-visual-content-in-your-marketing-data.aspx).

Chapter 4. Planning a Long-Term Content Strategy

1. 86% of highly effective organizations have someone steering the direction of their content strategy (http://neilpatel.com/2016/01/21/38-content-marketing-stats-that-every-marketer-needs-to-know/).

Chapter 5. Becoming an Effective Writer

1. On average, people consume 285 pieces of content or 54,000 words, every single day (http://www.marketingprofs.com/articles/2015/27698/2-million-blog-posts-are-written-every-day-heres-how-you-can-stand-out).
2. Eighty percent of people will read your headline, but only 20% will read the entire article (http://www.copyblogger.com/magnetic-headlines/).

Chapter 6. Creating a Blog Post

1. Moz's free title tag preview tool (https://moz.com/learn/seo/title-tag).

Chapter 7. Extending the Value of Your Content Through Repurposing

1. Of B2B marketers, 50% have an issue creating content on an ongoing basis (http://contentmarketinginstitute.com/wp-content/uploads/2016/09/2017_B2B_Research_FINAL.pdf).
2. When marketer and entrepreneur Ryan Battles publishes a blog post, he republishes it to LinkedIn, Medium, Reddit, and other relevant channels (https://ryanbattles.com/post/reposting-content).
3. HubSpot's free marketing resources library (https://www.hubspot.com/resources).
4. Seventy-nine percent of people said the cover was an important part of the decision-making process (http://thebooksmugglers.com/2010/04/cover-matters-the-survey-results.html).

Chapter 8. How to Effectively Promote Content

1. Of B2B buyers, 47% consume three to five pieces of content prior to engaging with a salesperson. (http://www.curata.com/blog/content-marketing-statistics-the-ultimate-list/).
2. Of B2B marketers, 42% say they're effective at content marketing. (http://contentmarketinginstitute.com/wp-content/uploads/2016/09/2017_B2B_Research_FINAL.pdf).

Chapter 9. Measuring and Analyzing Content

1. Eight percent of marketers consider themselves successful at tracking the performance of their content marketing efforts (https://www.hubspot.com/marketing-statistics).
2. Google Alerts: A tool to help you monitor the web for interesting, relevant content (https://www.google.com/alerts).
3. Google's Campaign URL builder (https://ga-dev-tools.appspot.com/campaign-url-builder/).

Chapter 10. Developing a Growth Marketing Mentality

1. Social media ad spend will likely exceed $35 billion in 2017, yet it only accounts for 13.9% of the total digital ad spend (https://blog.hootsuite.com/social-media-advertising-stats/).
2. Google receives over 90,000 search queries every second (http://searchengineland.com/google-now-handles-2-999-trillion-searches-per-year-250247).

Chapter 11. Creating Topic Clusters and Pillar Pages

1. Google's "Hummingbird" algorithm update in 2013 (http://searchengineland.com/google-hummingbird-172816).
2. Google's RankBrain algorithm update (http://searchengineland.com/faq-all-about-the-new-google-rankbrain-algorithm-234440).
3. The average first page ranking will also rank well for about 1,000 other relevant keywords (https://ahrefs.com/blog/also-rank-for-study/).
4. This page has hundreds of inbound links, most of which are sources mentioned on the page (https://majestic.com/reports/site-explorer?q=https%3A%2F%2Fwww.helpscout.net%2Fcustomer-acquisition%2F&oq=https%3A%2F%2Fwww.helpscout.net%2Fcustomer-acquisition%2F&IndexDataSource=F).

Index

Page numbers followed by *f* refer to figures.